THE JACK MANNING TRILOGY

DAVID WILLIAMSON's first full-length play, *The Coming of Stork*, premiered at the La Mama Theatre, Carlton, in 1970 and later became the film *Stork*, directed by Tim Burstall.

The Removalists and *Don's Party* followed in 1971, then *Jugglers Three* (1972), *What If You Died Tomorrow?* (1973), *The Department* (1975), *A Handful of Friends* (1976), *The Club* (1977) and *Travelling North* (1979). In 1972 *The Removalists* won the Australian Writers' Guild AWGIE Award for best stage play and the best script in any medium and the British production saw Williamson nominated most promising playwright by the London *Evening Standard*.

The 1980s saw his success continue with *Celluloid Heroes* (1980), *The Perfectionist* (1982), *Sons of Cain* (1985), *Emerald City* (1987) and *Top Silk* (1989); whilst the 1990s produced *Siren* (1990), *Money and Friends* (1991), *Brilliant Lies* (1993), *Sanctuary* (1994), *Dead White Males* (1995), *Heretic* (1996), *Third World Blues* (an adaptation of *Jugglers Three*) and *After the Ball* (both in 1997), *Corporate Vibes* and *Face to Face* (both in 1999); folowed by *The Great Man* (2000), *Up for Grabs, A Conversation* and *Charitable Intent* (all in 2001) and *Soulmates* (2002).

Williamson is widely recognised as Australia's most successful playwright and over the last thirty years his plays have been performed throughout Australia and produced in Britain, United States, Canada and many European countries. A number of his stage works have been adapted for the screen, including *The Removalists, Don's Party, The Club, Travelling North, Emerald City, Sanctuary* and *Brilliant Lies*.

David Williamson has won the Australian Film Institute film script award for *Petersen* (1974), *Don's Party* (1976), *Gallipoli* (1981) and *Travelling North* (1987) and has won eleven Australian Writers' Guild AWGIE Awards. He lives on Queensland's Sunshine Coast with his writer wife, Kristin Williamson.

From left: Geoff Cartwight as Jack, Amos Szeps as Barry and Duncan Young as Glen in the 1999 Ensemble Theatre production in Sydney of Face to Face. *(Photo: Geoff Beatty)*

DAVID WILLIAMSON

THE JACK MANNING TRILOGY
Face to Face
A Conversation
Charitable Intent

CURRENCY PRESS, SYDNEY

CURRENCY PLAYS

Face to Face first published in 1999
A Conversation first published in 2002
Charitable Intent first published in 2002
by Currency Press Pty Ltd,
Gadigal Land, Suite 310, 46–56 Kippax Street, Surry Hills, NSW 2010,
Australia
enquiries@currency.com.au
www.currency.com.au

Copyright © David Williamson, 2002.

COPYING FOR EDUCATIONAL PURPOSES
The Australian *Copyright Act 1968* (Act) allows a maximum of one chapter or 10% of this book, whichever is the greater, to be copied by any educational institution for its educational purposes provided that that educational institution (or the body that administers it) has given a remuneration notice to Copyright Agency Limited (CAL) under the Act.

For details of the CA licence for educational institutions contact CA, 12 / 66 Goulburn Street, Sydney, NSW, 2000. Tel: (02) 9394 7600; Fax: (02) 9394 7601; E-mail: memberservices@copyright.com.au

COPYING FOR OTHER PURPOSES
Except as permitted under the Act, for example a fair dealing for the purposes of study, research, criticism or review, no part of this book may be reproduced, stored in a retrieval system, or transmitted in any form or by any means without prior written permission. All inquiries should be made to the publisher at the address above.

Any performance or public reading of either *Face to Face*, *A Conversation* or *Charitable Intent* is forbidden unless a licence has been received from the author or the author's agent. The purchase of this book in no way gives the purchaser the right to perform the play in public, whether by means of a staged production or a reading. All applications for public performance should be addressed to the playwright c/- Cameron's Management, PO Box 848, Surry Hills NSW 2010, Australia; tel: within Australia 02 9319 7199; outside Australia +61 2 9319 7199; email: info@cameronsmanagement.com.au

In accordance with the requirement of the Australian Media, Entertainment & Arts Alliance, Currency Press has made every effort to identify, and gain permission of, the artists who appear in the photographs which illustrate these plays.

NATIONAL LIBRARY OF AUSTRALIA CIP DATA
   Williamson, David, 1942–.
      The Jack Manning trilogy.
      ISBN 0 86819 657 6.
      1. Mediation – Drama. 2. Criminals – Rehabilitation – Drama. 3.
      Victims of crime – Rehabilitation – Drama. I. Williamson, David, 1942–
      Face to face. II. Title.
   A822.3

Set by Dean Nottle
Cover design by Kate Florance
Front cover shows Guy Pearce as Jack Manning and Christine Stephen-Daly as Julie Rossiter in the 2000 Playbox Theatre production of *Face to Face*.
(Photo: Jeff Busby)

Contents

The Jack Manning Trilogy

A Justice That Heals   ix
David Williamson

The Theatre of Everyday Conflict   xvi
David Moore & John McDonald

Face to Face   1

A Conversation   53

Charitable Intent   105

Currency Press acknowledges the Traditional Owners of the Country on which we live and work. We pay our respects to all Aboriginal and Torres Strait Islander Elders, past and present.

A Justice That Heals

Conflict has both intrigued and worried me from my earliest days, a fact that's undoubtedly propelled me into my playwright's vocation. As the Greeks discovered, drama has got something to do with conflict. I grew up in a household where marital warfare was unceasing and endemic. There was never any physical violence between my parents but the bickering was intense. The legacy I have is a tendency to avoid conflict in real life. On the safety of the page, however, the causes of conflict and its consequences have continued to obsess me.

Several years back I got a letter from David Moore, an ex-academic who'd teamed up with John McDonald, a teacher turned policy adviser, to form Transformative Justice Australia. TJA is an organisation dedicated to introducing a radical new approach to conflict and justice—conferencing, or community conferencing. It's a technique that's designed to cope with the debilitating effects of conflict, paradoxically not by trying to wish that conflict away, but by letting it be forcefully expressed, then attempting to transform it. David and John were inspired by justice reforms in New Zealand, and, informed by a range of disciplines ranging from biology to organisational theory, they developed a circle-based process that could be applied to a wide range of conflicts. Less than ten years after its introduction it's a method that's gaining widespread acceptance in criminal, community and workplace situations, both in Australia and around the world.

The more I learnt of the dynamics of conferencing the more convinced I became that I wanted to use it as a basis for drama. I realised immediately that it would pose technical challenges. It is relatively easy to write a two-handed scene, but to write a whole play in which eight to ten characters are on stage and interact continuously is another matter. It wouldn't offer sets of visual splendour. Just a row of chairs in a semi-circle. And it wouldn't offer the kind of wall-banging stage hyperkinetics favoured by some directors. Physical movement would have to be replaced to some extent by emotional movement, although as conferencing allows people to get up and move around, a surprising amount of stage movement is still possible. Yet one of the problems for a dramatist in an Anglocentric society is that conflicts tend to be minimized in the social arena in order that we can all maintain a veneer of harmony. It was exciting for me to find authentic situations where real drama explodes with primal force through the barriers of social convention. As John, in his typical laconic way, said to me: 'Mate, I never have to go the theatre, I get full-on drama in my life every day'.

The other, no less exciting factor that drew me to this process was that it seemed to me then, and still does, a humane, effective and often moving method to reduce debilitating social conflict. As currently practised, conferencing is a micro-method of dealing with conflict, addressing itself to specific workplace, community and criminal situations in which conflict has caused physical and emotional harm. It offers no program for the overall restructuring of society, but it does offer a promise of change, both from the successive and cumulative impact of micro-environments made more harmonious, and even, perhaps in the future, in lessening society-wide conflicts which have become cyclically entrenched.

Finally what attracted me to the process is its optimistic take on humanity. At a time when talk of vengeance and retribution saturates our media, it's instructive to watch a community conference in action. Negative emotions *can* be transformed into positive ones. And not just fleetingly. The long-term outcomes are usually very good. A play or plays which depicted a typical conference and its outcome, I felt, might not only be effective drama, but could bring attention to a process that I believed in. And it might also help refute the ever growing ranks of cynics who ascribe to the Hobbesian view that human nature is irretrievably dark, egocentric and vengeful. Not that we aren't egocentric. Our cut finger means more to us than someone else's severed arm in a distant part of the globe. But conferencing relies on the fact that we are social creatures who crave the approval of others, and who have the capacity to be compassionate. Unless we are sociopathic, and only a small proportion of the population are, other people's distress causes us to feel distress. The core reason why this process works is that emotions are contagious. Anger elicits anger, happiness elicits happiness.

The Western intellectual tradition has for a long time been uncomfortable with the emotions. In glorifying the human intellect ('the thing that distinguishes us from animals'), it has shunned the emotions as an embarrassing relic of our biological past that served only to lead us into negative and destructive behaviour. If we could control these troublesome forces with logic and rationality, our lives would be much more fruitful.

Silvan S. Tomkins, an American philosopher and psychologist whose ideas date from the mid-1950s, reasoned quite differently. His thesis was that emotions are absolutely central to our existence. He re-read the insightful pioneering work on the emotions by Charles Darwin and realised that our basic affects—anger, fear, surprise, enjoyment/joy, distress/anguish, shame/guilt, disgust, contempt and interest/excitement—were an autonomous physiological response system common to all humankind.

When we become consciously aware that a physiological affect has been triggered we call it a feeling, and when an affect triggers conscious or unconscious memories of similar arousal in the past, we call it an emotion. Different cultures will teach their members to be angry, excited or disgusted at different things, but the affects themselves are universal. We tend to react to similar things. If someone steals our parking space, anger flares both in America and Japan. The Americans will simply express it more openly.

Tomkins' key insight, which excited me when I studied psychology in the 1970s just as it does today, was his answer to the ultimate question 'What is the purpose of life?', or, expressed a little less dramatically, 'How do we know what we want?'. To him, our lives were an attempt to maximise our experience of positive affect and minimise our experience of negative affect. We all try and get as much joy, contentment, and excitement; and as little anger, fear, distress, disgust and shame as we can. Our ultimate reward system is not money, or even love, but the emotions they engender. As Tomkins points out, however, our attempts to maximise our emotional rewards are usually very flawed because our knowledge of ourselves and our social context is always less than perfect. Conferencing attempts to give us a more accurate picture of ourselves and our social context in order to diminish our emotional pain and increase our emotional rewards. It takes participants through a transition from emotions like hate, fear, disgust and distress, into emotions at the more positive end of the spectrum. If not joy and excitement, then certainly interest, satisfaction and enjoyment.

Tomkins' theories have been given strong empirical validation by the recent work of neurophysiologists like Antonio Damasio and V.S. Ramachandran, whose detailed study of damage to key areas of the brain have established a much clearer picture of how the brain works. It is now known that conscious thought is much less important in motivation than the Western intellectual tradition would have us believe. In the words of David and John, 'Conscious thought is less a strategist that decides what we want; it is more a tactician that finds ways to get it'. Their book *Transforming Conflict*, summarises the advances in brain science, and illustrates the power of the limbic system, which controls the emotions. The limbic system decides which representations of reality are of emotional importance and will be acted on. If the cortex is damaged and loses its ability to refer to the limbic system for priorities, then alternative courses of action can no longer be sorted for their emotional significance. When this happens you get people who, while their intellect is functioning perfectly, are incapable of making decisions. Thus emotions, far from being disruptive outsiders to the intellect, are the crucial component of human decision making. When there is a lack of congruence in the brain between emotional information and cognitive or sensory information, emotional information always takes precedence. And the primacy of emotional information is the dynamic that drives conferencing.

In order to understand how conferencing is different from the mediation process often used as an alternative to the courtroom, it's necessary to understand the crucial distinction between a dispute and a conflict. A dispute is a situation in which the facts are in dispute. A conflict is a situation in which people feel negative emotions about each other. A dispute doesn't necessarily involve conflict, and a conflict can occur when there's no dispute.

The mediation process works best where there's a dispute. The procedures of mediation are expressly designed to minimise emotional arousal in order to prevent the dispute flaring into a conflict. The participants are encouraged to look at the facts rationally without letting their emotions become amplified or engaged. In a sense this method is the civilised heir of the western intellectual tradition of keeping the troublesome emotions in check, and often proves very effective, especially in cases in which the participants don't come harbouring strongly negative feelings about each other. However, if you've got a situation where people hate each other, then the facts of the dispute are not their prime concern. Disputes will arise from the smallest of pretexts as a result of the underlying conflict and if one dispute is solved another will be found to replace it. Where there is conflict, particularly severe conflict, disputes are only the symptom, not the cause, and mediation won't be effective.

At the other extreme, an unfortunate side effect of the courtroom process is that it tends to amplify conflict. Even if the participants arrive at court not feeling negatively about each other, the adversarial nature of the courtroom almost ensures negative feelings when they leave. The law is a zero sum game in which there is one winner and one loser. The awful legacy of rage that accompanies a court loss sometimes expresses itself in physical violence and even murder.

Conferencing works best in situations in which conflict is entrenched, and a circuit breaker is desperately needed to break the continuing spiral of retribution.

So how exactly does it work? What is the precise format, what stages does it go through, and how is conflict transformed?

Because we're egocentric creatures we tend to see the world from our viewpoint. When analyzing conflict we make ourselves the heroes and usually ascribe the worst motives to others. In truth, we're all a little paranoid and in a society that's becoming increasingly competitive and conflict prone, often more than a little. A conference situation allows all sides to see that the motives they imputed to others are often not their real motives, and, conversely, that their own actions have caused more emotional harm to others than they realised.

The first stage in the process is when a trained facilitator interviews all the potential conference participants to try and establish the key incidents in the ongoing conflict. Anything said by the participants is treated as confidential and may not be brought up at the conference by the facilitator.

The facilitator thus ascertains which incident or incidents are crucial and on the day of the conference will ask someone central to an incident to give his or her account of what happened. Others may then give their versions. The facilitator will steer the discussion, which at this stage is often full of anger, rage, fear and distress, towards the emotional and physical effects on everyone involved and the perpetrators will hear the extent of the damage they have wreaked. Most perpetrators will have minimised this damage in their own minds, so it is usually with surprise and eventually remorse that they discover how deeply other people have been affected. Their allies in the situation might also be surprised and put pressure on them to feel remorse. The perpetrators will then often explain their motives more fully than anyone in the group has ever heard. A supervisor for instance, might reveal the pressure from senior management to deliver greater productivity, and senior management, also present, might describe the threat of deteriorating market conditions on the business. Typically the genuine remorse expressed by the perpetrators leads to a crucial moment which David and John call 'collective vulnerability' when all the participants realise that they have misperceived the situation, and that, as a result, their community has suffered considerable emotional damage.

This is the crucial part of the conference, when the emotional negativity starts to be transformed. Genuine remorse elicits the beginning of genuine forgiveness and positive emotions come forth as people realise that negative outcomes can be changed. The vision of a community that can be healed and deliver positive emotional rewards excites them about the future.

The next stage of the conference is that the participants work out a contract between them so that the gains made during the conference can be continued into the future. The contract assigns responsibilities to various people and dates by which the actions will be met. The facilitator subsequently revisits the participants to check that the provisions of the contract have been honoured.

Sometimes after a conference some participants will begin to regret what they have revealed, thinking it will be of harm to their long-term prospects. David and John have found that such fears are misplaced. The honesty participants display is respected and after one or two months the full effects of the conference usually become apparent. The community or workplace delivers a much greater degree of emotionally rewarding experience for all.

David and John believe that the potential for conferencing will ultimately extend beyond the local community level to tackle intractable conflict between groups, or even nations, whose enduring hatreds are deep and atavistic. The present problem that occurs when leaders of two such nations negotiate a settlement is that their followers have no emotional investment in the settlement and rapidly break its terms. The optimism of the Oslo negotiations between Israel and Palestine was short-lived as extremists on both sides found new disputes to fuel their existing hatreds. If a conferencing process between leaders was televised so that the followers were drawn into the emotional power of the process, then they may feel more part of the contract their leaders have negotiated.

But that's for the future. In the present, the methods pioneered by these two extraordinary Australians continue to be exported to the world.

David Williamson
2001

The Theatre of Everyday Conflict

In April 1998, a review article by David Williamson appeared in the Australian newspaper's monthly *Review of Books*. The article, entitled 'Mixed Feelings', offered a succinct overview of key debates about emotionality. It struck a chord with us. So we wrote David a letter. He phoned back. We had lunch and a fascinating conversation began. It seemed only a matter of months before a draft of *Face to Face* was in the (e-)mail. Even in first draft, *Face to Face* powerfully portrayed the essence of a TJA Conference in a heavy industrial workplace.

The TJA conference is a structured conversation in a community of people affected by conflict. It is one of several processes designed to transform the negative emotions associated with conflict into the positive emotions associated with co-operation. The idea sounds simple, but as Directors of Transformative Justice Australia (TJA), we had long wrestled with the question of how to convey the principles behind the practice. Even more difficult is to convey to a wider audience the living experience of this emotional transformation. David's radical naturalist plays seem to answer both these questions.

The typical 'real' TJA Conference in a workplace will last for quite a few hours. But *Face to Face* compresses all the crucial turning points, the low points and high points, into an hour and a half of theatre. And a powerful hour and a half it is. With ten actors on stage throughout, no breaks and no scene changes, the play must be carried by raw emotions. And it was this topic that brought practitioners and playwright together.

We had the privilege of watching David at work researching *Face to Face*. He participated in a TJA Conference facilitator's workshop— where he performed admirably in the role plays. He also observed us facilitating workplace conferences, and talked through some of our case studies at length. The resulting play compresses these experiences into a drama remarkably close to the experience of being inside the circle.

To achieve this compression, David has Jack Manning play an additional role of commentator on the process. Jack paraphrases and offers suggestions to participants more as commentator than facilitator. Technically, these interventions diverge from some of our own groundrules or guidelines for conference facilitation. But this proves a clever dramatic device. And in the original production directed by Sandra Bates of Sydney's Ensemble Theatre, Jeff Cartwright played Jack Manning's dual role with a voice that toggled between engagement and the more detached commentary of a radio broadcaster.

Importantly, the facilitator-as-commentator clearly upholds the general principles of a truly democratic process: everyone affected participates in the process, their voices all count, issues are appropriately deliberated, and no one is allowed to tyrannise others. Again, the dramatist underscores this principle of non-tyranny. Every participant has their moment that prompts pin-drop silence. And everyone at some stage prompts laughter. It's the laughter of recognition from an audience only one step removed from this workplace drama. This is emotion in the raw because it's life in the raw. Structured so that we neither minimise conflict nor maximise it. We confront it and transform it. Here we do so in the theatre, one of the original sites of transformation.

The success of *Face to Face* in the theatre created a challenge. Could another play about TJA Conferencing achieve the same raw power, balancing tragedy and comedy with a sense of intellectually justifiable optimism? In 2001, David Williamson answered that challenge not once but twice. The premieres of *A Conversation* at Sydney's Ensemble and *Charitable Intent* at Melbourne's La Mama received at least as much popular and critical acclaim as *Face to Face*. Writing in the *Australian*, theatre critic John McCallum urged David to render the title of this 'trilogy' inaccurate by writing fourth and fifth instalments.

With *A Conversation* and *Charitable Intent*, David showed empathically that *Face to Face* was not simply a vehicle to dramatise the version of conferencing developed by the TJA through the 1990s. Rather, as in the world outside the theatre, conferencing on the stage provides a vehicle through which a group of people in bitter conflict might reach a deeper and shared understanding of how that conflict developed. In their moment of greatest collective vulnerability, they consider how to work together towards a brighter future. In each of these plays David poses some specific and hard questions about the TJA Conferencing process.

In *Face to Face*, the simplicity of the basic story raises a technical question about TJA Conferencing in the workplace. The dismissed employee, Glen, assaulted a colleague and rammed the boss's Mercedes. These are harmful acts. There is *no* dispute about that. And undisputed harm of this nature—criminal damage and assault—is generally dealt with in the justice system, not in workplaces. Conferencing in workplaces deals, more typically, with *many* disputes. Each dispute is a mere symptom of growing conflict (which is commonly and confusingly called 'declining morale'). So a technical question addressed in *Face to Face* is whether Conferencing is appropriate in workplaces where there is no dispute about a specific act that has caused widespread harm. An unforgettable hour and a half of theatre answers: yes.

A Conversation deals with a far more devastating crime. Again, the play's basic story is stark in its simplicity. The families of the two parties in a brutal rape and murder are brought together in a TJA Conference. Equally stark are the questions that this raises: what is to be gained when everything has been lost? What outcome could possibly make things better? And is it still a conference if the primary victim can't attend for obvious reasons, and the jailed offender, who appears to be genuinely psychopathic, won't attend? The answers, as with so much about Conferencing, seem paradoxical. One father told us that a Conference held after his son's murder helped him and others gain a 'shared understanding' that made it possible to continue with life. The father in another of the cases that inspired *A Conversation* told us that 'the *process* is the outcome'. And *A Conversation* reminds audiences that a conference is not held for any particular individual. Each person touched by the conflict has equally valid reasons for participating.

Charitable Intent likewise raises questions about the Conferencing process. As we discussed with David during his typically intense preparation for writing, TJA Conferences often reveal the complexity of situations, and that complexity tends to make people's actions more understandable. But what if conflict really has been generated not by complex set of events, but by a clear clash between cultures? And what if, the more complex a story becomes, the more clearly one person seems to be at odds with the culture of the group? What if that person really is the uncomplicated bully they first appeared to be?

Like the first two plays in the trilogy, *Charitable Intent* poses the question of whether Conferencing is appropriate for a particular type of case. And again the answer is a convincing: yes. But the play offers no simple happy ending. As critics observed, not everyone experiences personal transformation during this clash between community sector and corporate sector cultures. Some people just leave. So be it: something was learned, people move on; an untenable situation seems to be changed for the better.

Despite their differences, then, all three plays dramatise the transformation of conflict into cooperation. And in a fascinating development, the premiere of the plays was paralleled by significant transformations in systems that deal with conflict. For example, after David had penned *A Conversation*, but before the play opened at the Ensemble Theatre, the Minister for Corrections in New South Wales announced that a successful pilot of TJA Conferencing in corrections would be extended statewide. Anyone involved in a case where a court had imposed a sentence could apply to participate in a conference with the other people affected.

Around the same time, one-off performance readings of *A Conversation* were moving audiences in the US. In Philadelphia, where TJA Conferencing has been introduced to workplaces through the Comey Institute of Industrial Relations, David and Kristin Williamson attended a performance of *A Conversation* to the riveted members of an Hispanic North Philadelphia neighbourhood. In Baltimore, where our colleague Lauren Abramson has established a successful and busy Community Conferencing Center, the first of its kind in the US, people were similarly moved. And across the Atlantic, also in 2001, the British Home Office agreed to fund a major randomised controlled trial of conferencing at all stages of the justice system. We were completing the second round of training for UK conference facilitators just as David's new plays premiered in Sydney and Melbourne.

As more than one critic pointed out, these were the fifth and sixth plays from David's pen in less than three years. More prolific than ever, he remains as perceptive as ever about which big issues, now, will remain big issues in years to come. With these three plays, he has dramatised a more constructive approach to the sort of conflict that affects us all at some stage in our lives.

There has been an appropriate symbolism in these plays being staged in parallel with the likes of *Corporate Vibes*, *The Great Man* and *Up for Grabs*. These rapidly moving plays satirise excesses of political and financial power, with a format that David perfected through the 1980s and 1990s. *The Jack Manning Trilogy*, more about a process than a person, represents a different aesthetic and ethic. Here there is more laughing *with* people than at them. And there are tears. But above all, there is change, and most of it is for the better, because the people most affected by the drama are given a say over the things that matter most to them. They retain their dignity. In that commitment to genuine democracy, we can recognise the same old David Williamson who, in October 2001, returned to La Mama, thirty years after *The Coming of Stork*. *Charitable Intent*, along with the rest of the *Trilogy*, carried a message that is unchanged at one level, new at another, and profoundly important.

David Moore
for Transformative Justice Australia
Sydney

Face to Face

Damien Richardson as Glen in the 2000 Playbox Theatre production in Melbourne. (Photo: Jeff Busby)

Face to Face was first produced by the Ensemble Theatre at the Ensemble Theatre, Sydney, on 20 March 1999, with the following cast:

JACK MANNING	Geoff Cartwright
GLEN TREGASKIS	Duncan Young
MAUREEN TREGASKIS	Carol Willesee
BARRY MCLEAN	Amos Szeps
GREG BALDONI	Barry Langrishe
CLAIRE BALDONI	Sharon Flanigan
RICHARD HALLIGAN	Ian Bolt
LUKA MITROVIC	Andrew Doyle
JULIE ROSSITER	Danielle Carter
THERESE MARTIN	Lauren Clair

Director, Sandra Bates
Production manager, Melissa Gray
Assistant to the Director, Kathryn Oakman

CHARACTERS

JACK MANNING, community conference convenor
GLEN TREGASKIS, mid-20s
MAUREEN TREGASKIS, early 40s, Glen's mother
BARRY MCLEAN, mid-20s, Glen's friend
GREG BALDONI, early 50s, owner and manager of Baldoni Exhibition Constructions
CLAIRE BALDONI, Greg's wife
RICHARD HALLIGAN, 40s, foreman at Baldoni's
LUKA MITROVIC, early 30s, Baldoni's employee
JULIE ROSSITER, Greg's presonal assistant at Baldoni's
THERESE MARTIN, Greg's accountant

Nine people, three on one side, six on the other, sit in horseshoe formation facing the audience. The convenor, JACK MANNING, *sits at the centre of the horseshoe facing the audience.*

JACK: Hi. As you all know by now, my name's Jack Manning, and I'll be convening this community conference. Before we start let's introduce everyone. You all know Glen Tregaskis.

> GLEN, *a large, powerfully-built man in his middle twenties, barely looks up as he's acknowledged.*

Some of you mightn't know his mother, Maureen.

> MAUREEN, *an attractive slim woman in her early forties, sitting next to her son, nods anxiously.*

Or Barry McLean, a long-time friend of Glen's, from right back in their primary school days.

> BARRY, *about the same age as* GLEN *and wearing a bikie jacket, nods.*

Greg Baldoni, the owner and manager of Baldoni Exhibition Constructions, and his wife Claire.

> GREG, *a man in his early fifties, athletic-looking and well-dressed, nods. His wife* CLAIRE, *attractive, slim, well-dressed and well-groomed, barely moves.*

Two of Glen's workmates, Richard Halligan and Luka Mitrovic.

> RICHARD *and* LUKA, *sitting near the Baldonis, nod.* RICHARD *is in his forties,* LUKA *is in his early thirties.*

Greg's personal assistant, Julie Rossiter, and his accountant, Therese Martin.

> JULIE *beams a big smile at all who will receive it.* THERESE *nods in an embarrassed fashion.*

Thanks to all of you for making the effort to come. This is a difficult matter, but the fact that you're all here together will help us work out how you want to handle it. We're going to try and focus on the incident itself, which happened outside Greg's house at five past six on Tuesday the ninth of June, and which involved Greg and

Glen. We want to see how all the people involved have been affected, and our aim will be to try and see whether we can begin to repair the harm that's been done. [*He turns and looks at* GLEN.] Glen, you've admitted being involved in the incident. If you don't want to continue being here you're free to leave at any stage. But if you do leave, then you'll probably have to face a normal courtroom trial. You're clear about that?

GLEN, *head down, nods.*

Glen, could you start this conference by telling us all what happened?

GLEN *doesn't respond.*

Step by step.

GLEN: Youse all know already.

JACK: We'd like to hear it from you. Exactly how you remember it.

GLEN: [*indicating* GREG] I rammed his bloody Mercedes. Went right up his arse with my bullbar. Crumpled like cardboard.

JACK: Where did this happen?

GLEN: Outside his house.

JACK: How did you come to be there?

GLEN: I went there. After he sacked me.

JACK: Straight after he sacked you?

GLEN: No. I had a few drinks first.

JACK: How many?

GLEN: A few.

JACK: Would you say you were drunk, Glen?

GLEN: No.

JACK: Would you say you were sober?

GLEN: No.

JACK: Sort've halfway.

GLEN: Yeah.

JACK: So after a few drinks you went to Greg's house. Was he there?

GLEN: No. Hadn't arrived back from work.

JACK: So?

GLEN: Parked opposite, waited till he pulled into his drive and went right up his arse with me bullbar.

JACK: What were you feeling at the time?

GLEN: Great. Crumpled like bloody cardboard.

JACK: Before you hit him.

GLEN: Pissed off.
JACK: What do you reckon about it now?
GLEN: I reckon anybody who buys a Mercedes is crazy. Crumpled like cardboard.
JACK: Do you still feel good that you did it?
GLEN: No.
JACK: Why not?
GLEN: Wasn't smart.
JACK: Who's been affected by what you did, Glen?
GLEN: My mum.
JACK: How did it affect your mum?
GLEN: Made her upset.
JACK: How do you feel about that?
GLEN: Not great.
JACK: You care about your mum?
GLEN: She's had a rough enough time without this sort of shit.
JACK: Anyone else affected?
GLEN: Me sister. She's still so mad at me she wouldn't come today.
MAUREEN: She just couldn't face this sort of thing.
JACK: Anyone else affected, Glen?
GLEN: No, mainly Mum.

There's a silence. JACK *looks at him, then across at* GREG.

JACK: There's no one else here that's been affected by what you did?

There's another silence. GLEN *shakes his head.*

GREG: What's the use?

JACK *ignores the intervention, his gaze remaining on* GLEN.

[*To* GLEN] You don't think I was affected?
JACK: Do you think Mr Baldoni was affected, Glen?
GLEN: Yeah, he hurt his neck a bit.
GREG: A bit? It's only just come out of a brace.
JACK: Was ramming the car all you did to Mr Baldoni that day, Glen?
GLEN: Yeah.

JACK *anticipates that* GREG *may intervene so he holds up his hand in* GREG*'s direction without taking his gaze off* GLEN.

I rammed his car. That's all.
JACK: You said something to Mr Baldoni, didn't you?

GLEN: I might've.
GREG: He said if I didn't give him his job back he'd wait till I got my Merc repaired and do it again. And again.
JACK: Did you say that, Glen?
GLEN: Might've. Can't remember much.
JACK: Did you really think saying that would help you get your job back?
GLEN: Must've or I wouldn't've done it.
JACK: What do you think now?
GLEN: Not a great move. I still want my job back, but.
JACK: Do you think that's likely, Glen?
GLEN: That's why I come here today. It's the only job I ever bloody liked. It's the only job I've ever been bloody good at, [*pointing to* GREG] and he gives me the shove.
JACK: Glen, do you think it's likely that Mr Baldoni *will* give you your job back again?
BARRY: [*indicating* GLEN] Give him a break, mate!

    JACK *ignores* BARRY *and keeps his gaze fixed on* GLEN.

GLEN: [*to* JACK] You got a job, haven't ya? Eh? You do this sort of shit. You got no worries. How would you like it if someone took your bloody job away?!

    GLEN *is clearly upset. He wipes away tears of anger from his eyes.*

BARRY: Give him a break, mate!

    JACK *looks briefly at* BARRY *with a look of reprimand, then turns his attention back to* GLEN.

JACK: Glen, how do you think Mr Baldoni felt when you rammed his car and threatened him?
GLEN: Dunno. He just sat there.
JACK: How do you *think* he was feeling?
GLEN: How would I bloody know?! He didn't say a thing.
JACK: Why do you think that was?
GLEN: I dunno.
BARRY: Lay off, mate. You're giving him the third bloody degree.
JACK: Barry. Glen, mate, I think you can probably guess how Mr Baldoni was feeling, can't you?

GLEN: I hate lots of questions. It gets me mad and I get confused.
BARRY: He gets stirred up about things. He's not stupid, he just gets stirred up.
GLEN: Thanks mate.
BARRY: [*to* GLEN] Calm down, mate.
JACK: Glen, you can leave if you want to, but you did agree to come.
GLEN: I jus' want me bloody job back! That's why I come here!
JACK: I'm not sure that's why everyone else is here.
RICHARD: Glen, mate, if someone waited outside your place and rammed your car, how would you feel?
GLEN: I'd be laughin', mate. I've been wanting the insurance on that heap for years.
JACK: Glen, Mr Baldoni had just bought his Mercedes. Do you think he was laughing?
GLEN: Didn't look like it.
JACK: How do you think he was feeling?
GLEN: A bit pissed off I guess.
JACK: Just a bit.
GLEN: He's insured. Lose his no claim, but he's filthy rich so it's not a big deal, is it?

There's a pause.

JACK: Let's find out how Greg feels about it. [*He turns to* GREG.] Greg, what did you feel at the time?
GREG: What do you think? When you're just turning into your drive you're maybe entitled to think you're home. You're safe. You can relax. You're not exactly expecting to be rammed from the rear. You're not exactly expecting to be shouted at when you're still in shock.
JACK: How do you feel about it all now?
GREG: I still feel very angry. The whole thing wasn't my fault. I had no other option but to fire him. I gave him a job when nobody else would and who could blame them, given his track record? Good God, I've been so bloody tolerant up to now. It's not the first time he's attacked his workmates.
JACK: Now hang on, Greg. I was given to understand from Richard that Glen hadn't actually attacked anyone before. Not since he'd been working for you.

GREG: He certainly threatened people before. He was screaming at Nookie for ten minutes out in the yard there one day.

JACK: But he didn't attack him.

GREG: It was only a matter of time. But every time there was a flare-up it was the same bloody story. 'Don't fire him. He'll never get another job.'

JACK: Who urged you not to sack him?

GREG: [*pointing to* RICHARD] Richard. My foreman. And he's the one who finally got hit.

JACK: [*to* RICHARD] You thought Glen would be okay.

RICHARD: Basically he's a very hard worker. The best of the lot of them in terms of enthusiasm and energy.

GLEN: First to arrive, last to leave. Every bloody day.

RICHARD: He was so bloody enthusiastic he was a pain. He'd turn up half an hour before starting time and leap around saying, 'Where are the buggers? Let's get going. Let's get going.' When a foreman gets a guy like that you don't exactly want to sack him. [*Pause.*] I knew he had a track record of punching people out, but I thought I could handle all that.

GLEN: I only fight when someone picks me!

JACK: You've got a reputation for getting along with people, haven't you Richard?

RICHARD: I get on with most people.

JACK: You said you actually felt good about the fact that you were getting on well with a guy who no one else would employ.

GLEN: I only fight people who pick me!

RICHARD: Up to the time he turned on me I liked him. Most of the time he's good humoured. Full of fun.

JACK: [*turning to* CLAIRE] You were at home on the day of the incident, Claire?

CLAIRE: Yes.

JACK: You heard the crash.

CLAIRE: [*nodding*] I ran outside and saw Glen screaming abuse at Greg through the window.

JACK: How did you feel?

CLAIRE: Totally shocked.

JACK: Did you know who Glen was?

CLAIRE: I had no idea.

JACK: How do you think it's affected you both?
CLAIRE: It's been appalling. Greg still can't sleep. We both can't. You had to be there to know what it was like. The car was wrecked and Glen was just screaming. Screaming. It really was like a nightmare. Still is.
JACK: Glen, Claire's just told you how it affected her. What do you think now?

He looks at GLEN. GLEN *shifts his gaze.*

Glen, you've had your joke. You told us that if someone suddenly bashed into your car you'd be glad. The insurance and all that. If someone rammed you from behind with no warning, can you tell us how you'd really feel?
BARRY: Give him a break.
CLAIRE: Barry, this whole conference was set up to give him a break.
JACK: Glen, you're just turning into your driveway and someone deliberately rams your car. How do you feel?
GLEN: Not great I guess.
JACK: Claire, can you tell us again how it's affected you both?
CLAIRE: Greg was in pain for weeks. He still can't sleep. Neither can I.
JACK: Has the physical pain been the worst part, Greg?
GREG: I guess.

JACK stares at him steadily, not satisfied with the answer. The silence grows.

CLAIRE: He's been a nervous wreck. We get phone calls and no one answers.
JACK: Do you know anything about these calls, Glen?

Again there's a silence. JACK *keeps his gaze focussed on* GLEN *who looks away.*

GLEN: Yeah.
JACK: You didn't tell me that when you talked to me.
GLEN: I don't want to hurt them. I jus' want to ask for me job back, but when they answer I can't think of what to say.
JACK: Should have told me, Glen.
GLEN: Yeah.
JACK: Can you understand how phone calls like that might affect people, Glen?
GLEN: I'm not gonna touch him again. I jus' want me bloody job back.

JACK: Can you understand how upset you've made Mr and Mrs Baldoni?
GLEN: I'm more upset than they are.
JACK: Yes, you're upset, but so are they. And right now we're trying to focus on them. Can you understand that they're more upset than you maybe thought they were?
GLEN: Yeah.
JACK: Is there anything you want to say to them?

GLEN *stays silent.* JACK *keeps looking at him.*

GLEN: Richard told you how good I was at my job but Mr Baldoni still sacked me.
JACK: That's all you want to say, Glen?
GLEN: They might be upset but they're not as upset as me!
JACK: All right. Let's come back to that a little later. Maureen, what were your first thoughts when you heard about this?
MAUREEN: My stomach turned over. For the first time in his life Glen has a job he loves, and he's happy, and all of a sudden, without any warning, it's all over.

From left: Damien Richardson as Glen, Gina Gaigalas as Maureen, Andrea Swifte as Claire, Scott Gooding as Barry and Guy Pearce as Jack in the 2000 Playbox Theatre production in Melbourne. (Photo: Jeff Busby)

JACK: Without any warning? You hadn't heard about the flare-ups?

MAUREEN: Yes, Greg phoned me once and told me Glen'd shouted at Nookie, and to speak to him about it, and I did and I thought everything would be okay.

JACK: What caused the flare-up with—is it Nookie?

RICHARD: Nookie. Yeah. Nookie Finlay's a pretty tough nut and he likes to needle people, and Glen's always a bit of a target.

JACK: Why's that?

RICHARD: He chatters on. He doesn't mean any harm, but he can be annoying because a lot of it's just bull.

GLEN: No it's not!

RICHARD: You exaggerate things a bit, Glen. That's all I mean. Nookie likes to bait people and you always rise to the bait.

GLEN: Nookie's a shit.

RICHARD: I wouldn't disagree with you, mate.

JACK: I tried to get Nookie here today, but he wouldn't come.

RICHARD: Nookie isn't interested in solving problems, just starting them.

JACK: For whatever reason it was pretty heavy, this shouting match with Nookie?

RICHARD: Not too bad. Nookie always backs down if his hide is threatened.

JACK: It was serious enough for you to tell Mr Baldoni, and serious enough for Mr Baldoni to phone Maureen and tell her to try and get it into Glen's head that he had to control his temper. Right Greg?

GREG: Absolutely. Maureen worked for me a few years back. I just thought a quiet call might help. And it seemed to.

MAUREEN: I knew things weren't perfect, but on balance it was working out better than it ever had before.

JACK: Glen's temper has been a long-term problem, hasn't it?

MAUREEN: Glen's got a quick fuse. Everyone knows that. He was never an Einstein at school, and he's always had a quick fuse, but he's always been a friendly and willing boy too. That's what some people forget. He loves work. Always has. Ask him to do something and it was done. He'd do anything for anyone who treats him right.

BARRY: [*nodding*] Do anything for his mates.

MAUREEN: Glen's too trusting. He gets picked on. Teased.

JACK: How long did he last in his other jobs?

MAUREEN: When you're provoked you strike out. It's only human.
JACK: How long did he keep these jobs?
MAUREEN: Not long. But this one was different.
JACK: So what finally went wrong this time, Glen? Why *did* Greg fire you?
GLEN: I jobbed Richard.
JACK: Why?
GLEN: He can tell you.

  JACK *turns and looks at* RICHARD.

RICHARD: I was the only one stupid enough to be still around when Glen found out the others had set him up.
MAUREEN: They made a total fool of him.
LUKA: It was just a bloody joke.
MAUREEN: Some joke.
JACK: It was a joke that'd been going on for quite a while, hadn't it Richard?
LUKA: For Christ's sake, everyone takes the piss out of everyone else. That's the only way we get through the bloody day. You ever tried erecting scaffolding ten hours a day, six days a week?
RICHARD: We rib each other all the time.
LUKA: You get some shit, you dish it back.
RICHARD: It was just a joke.
BARRY: Big joke.
LUKA: Look, who the fuck do you think you are?
BARRY: I'm his oldest mate.
LUKA: Lucky you. We work with him.
JACK: Luka, perhaps you'd better tell us about this 'joke'.
LUKA: Everyone here knows.
JACK: Julie, you had a part in all this ah—'joke', didn't you?
LUKA: For God's sake, it *was* a bloody joke.
JACK: You tell us about it then, Luka.
LUKA: From the minute he arrived he was telling us how strong he was, how fit he was. How he could lift twice as much as any of us.
GLEN: I could.
LUKA: How women were crazy about him. Drove us bloody mad.
GLEN: I didn' say that. I said a lot of girls thought I looked like Mel Gibson, an' it's true. Jus' couldn' take it.

RICHARD: If you believed what Glen told you, he was God's gift to women.
LUKA: Told us fifty times that some tart told him he looked like Mel Gibson.
GLEN: She did. And she weren't a tart. And she weren't the only one.
BARRY: Calm down, mate.
JULIE: It was just a joke. The boys came to me and said that Glen thought he was Mel Gibson and to play up to him a bit.
JACK: Who came to you, Julie?
JULIE: Luka.
LUKA: It was just a joke.
JACK: So what happened?
JULIE: Every time he came into the office, or I went out into the yard, I'd give him a bit of a look and a smile.
JACK: What'd he do?
JULIE: Just went bright red.
GLEN: They were jus' having me on, Barry.
BARRY: Calm down, mate. It's okay. We're gonna get to the bottom of it.
JACK: [*to* LUKA] So what happened then?
LUKA: What do you think? We told him she had the hots for him and to go for it.
JACK: What did you do, Glen?
GLEN: Bastards.
JACK: What did you do?
GLEN: I asked Luka to ask her for me.
JACK: Ask her what?
GLEN: Whether she wanted to go to the flicks wif me.
JACK: What did you tell Glen, Luka?
GLEN: They told me to go right into the city and she'd meet me outside Village. They told me she wanted to see *Godzilla*. Y'know. 'Size matters'. I wanted to see it too.
JACK: And she didn't turn up.
GLEN: No. I was so mad I didn't even see it. Still haven't.
BARRY: It's shit, mate. Don't bother.
JACK: What happened when you turned up to work on Monday?
GLEN: Luka told me she already had a boyfriend and she was scared she'd fall in love wif me and he'd get mad.

JACK: So what'd you do?
GLEN: I told him to tell her not to worry. I'd beat shit outta the bastard if he gave her any trouble. He come back and told me that she'd meet me at the dogs, 'cause her boyfriend never went there.
JACK: You like greyhound racing, Glen?
GLEN: Yeah, I love the dogs, but she didn't show up again.
JACK: How'd you feel?
GLEN: Pretty pissed. I told Barry and me mates that she was turning up and she didn't.
JACK: Did you and your mates think it was very likely that anyone was going to turn up, Barry?
BARRY: We guessed it was some sorta joke.
JACK: But you didn't tell Glen that?
BARRY: Didn't have the heart.
JACK: So what did Glen do when she didn't turn up?
BARRY: He told us about this boyfriend. We told him we'd take care of the boyfriend.
JACK: So you played along.
BARRY: It was just a bit of fun.
JACK: So Glen gives you and your mates a bit of 'fun' from time to time too?
BARRY: We kid him along sometimes. Nothing sick like these pricks did.
JACK: You encourage him to tell the story about how the girl told him he looks like Mel Gibson?
GLEN: She did!
BARRY: It's harmless, mate.
JACK: Yeah, okay. So what'd you do when you got back to work on Monday this time, Glen?
GLEN: I fronted her m'self, this time. I told her she made me look like a dickhead in fronta me mates.
JACK: What did you do, Julie?
JULIE: I felt a bit guilty and told him that I hadn't told the whole truth. I told him that I was flattered that a guy as handsome as he was, was fond of me, but that I really did love my boyfriend and that I was sorry.
JACK: How did that go down?
JULIE: Okay. He seemed fine.

LUKA: Then he nearly drove us mad telling us that Julie told him she was crazy for him and that she was going to ditch her boyfriend any second now. So we told him that the one who was really crazy about him was Therese.
JACK: How did he react to that?
LUKA: He said Therese was too quiet for him, but we told him that the quiet ones were the ones who really go for it.
JACK: So what happened, Therese?
THERESE: [*edgily*] He started coming in the office and looking at me.
JACK: How did you feel?
THERESE: Upset. [*Pause.*] I don't handle that sort of thing very well. [*Looking at* JULIE] I'm not the social type like some around here. I liked Glen. He was always cheerful. But not in *that* sort of way.
JACK: Did he become a nuisance?
THERESE: At the start he only looked and smiled. Don't get me wrong. I'm not a nun or anything. I like being noticed. But I didn't want Glen to think that I liked him in that sort of way.
JACK: What did you do when he smiled at you?
THERESE: I just looked the other way.
GLEN: They tol' me she did that to everyone. They tol' me that meant she was hot for me. They tol' me to write her a letter.
JACK: And Luka helped you write it?
LUKA: It was a joke.
GLEN: An' they said she wrote one back, but she didn't. Julie wrote it.
JULIE: I didn't think it was going to cause any trouble.
JACK: [*to* GLEN] It told you to meet Therese in the carpark at lunchtime and she'd take you to the place she has lunch?
GLEN: It was bullshit. Julie wrote it 'cause Luka told her to.
JACK: [*to* JULIE] Didn't you think Therese might have been frightened?
JULIE: It was a bit of a joke on Therese as well.
JACK: Why did you want to play a joke on Therese?
JULIE: She can be a bit off-putting. When you talk to her she turns her head away and just says yes or no without even looking at you.
THERESE: I don't *want* to be like that.

There's a pause. JACK *keeps focussed on* THERESE.

I don't want to be like that. It's just that everything I say sounds stupid as soon as I've said it.
JACK: [*to* LUKA] The joke went a bit sour?

THERESE: I got frightened. He tried to get in my car.
GLEN: They told me she might try and back out of it. They told me 'just do it'.
GREG: The first I heard about it Therese comes running into the office crying. Glen came after her. I twigged to what'd happened straight away.
JACK: From what you said to me, Greg, Richard had kept you up to date on this long-running 'joke' and you were quite amused. Up to this point.
GREG: There didn't seem much harm in it. Frankly anything that keeps the lads amused helps stop their whingeing. But when I saw the state Therese was in, I knew it'd gone too far. I told Glen his mates had played a trick on him and when he went off after them I phoned Richard on his mobile and told them to make themselves scarce. Luka and the others got to hell out of there.
RICHARD: It wasn't me who set this thing up, so I thought I was safe to stay.
GLEN: You were in on it too! [*To* JACK] They were all bloody in on it.
JACK: [*to* GLEN] You beat up Richard.
GLEN: He was in on it too!
RICHARD: I knew about it, but it wasn't me who was doing it.
JACK: But you were the one who copped it.
RICHARD: I was the only one around.
JACK: Did you mean to hurt him as badly as you did, Glen?
GLEN: He was in on it too!
JACK: Do you think he was the main one?
GLEN: Luka was the main one, but Luka had pissed off.
GREG: We thought at first we'd have to get an ambulance for Richard. He looked a mess.
JACK: When did you tell Glen he was fired?
GREG: As soon as we'd cleaned up Richard. Glen was locked in his car in the carpark. He said that if I sacked him he'd go and drive his car into a tree. I told him I had no other option and he just turned on the ignition and burned off.
JACK: What did you do then?
MAUREEN: He rang me and I was worried out of my wits. I knew Glen wouldn't kill himself, because he always threatened to do it but never did, but I was worried.

GREG: Then I drove home.
JACK: [*to* GLEN] How do you feel now about what you did to Richard?
GLEN: Pretty bad. It shoulda been Luka.
JACK: Do you think there's anything you should say to Richard?

> GLEN *hangs his head. There's a pause. The pause extends.*

GLEN: Sorry mate. Shoulda been Luka.
RICHARD: It's okay, mate. No permanent damage.
GLEN: [*with real feeling*] Sorry mate.

> *He has tears in his eyes. He gets up and moves across to* RICHARD *and hugs him.*

Sorry mate. You were the best of the lot of 'em. And I have to go and job you.
RICHARD: I'm the bloody foreman. I knew what was going on. I should've stopped it.
GLEN: You were the best of the lot of them.
RICHARD: I thought it was just a joke.

> GLEN *gives* RICHARD *a last hug and goes back to his seat. There's a silence.*

LUKA: I wasn't the only one in on it, for God's sake.
MAUREEN: You were the ring leader.
LUKA: I never did any of the other stuff. I never borrowed money off him like some of his other workmates.
MAUREEN: Workmates? They weren't his mates. None of them. Bled him dry every pay day. Took him drinking and made him shout them all.
RICHARD: We didn't make him, Mrs Tregaskis. He always insisted.
GLEN: Mum, I shouted 'cause I wanted to. I'm not mean.
MAUREEN: Sometimes he'd come home with half his pay packet gone. What he didn't shout he 'lent'. It wasn't *lending*, it was robbery.
GLEN: Mum, they were me mates.
MAUREEN: Some mates.
RICHARD: I didn't ever borrow from him. I let him buy me a beer or two but I didn't borrow.
LUKA: Neither did I.
MAUREEN: You took more than one or two drinks. You all did.
RICHARD: It made him happy.
GLEN: Mum, they were me mates.

MAUREEN: I used to cry in bed at nights over what they did to him.
BARRY: Bloody animals. You'll get yours, Luka!
LUKA: I didn't rob him like some of the others!
GLEN: Mum, it was okay.
MAUREEN: They used to set him up for their bloody amusement. Set him onto other guys in the pub. Get him into fights. I used to cry at night over what they did to him. Poor kid. No defences. Trust anyone. They just used him as a butt for their amusement.
GLEN: Mum! You're making me sound a real idiot.
BARRY: If I had've known what was going on we woulda sorted you guys out.
LUKA: Of course you guys never got him into any trouble at the bloody dogs or wherever, did you?
GLEN: Mum. You're makin' me sound like a real idiot.
MAUREEN: [*putting an arm around his shoulder*] You're not an idiot, son. You just trust people you shouldn't.
GLEN: They're me mates.
MAUREEN: [*with tears in her eyes*] Absolutely defenceless. Not one skerrick of remorse. Took half his pay packet week after week. Got him into fights just to get a cheap laugh.
RICHARD: I didn't approve of that stuff.
MAUREEN: [*angrily*] You didn't do anything to stop it though, did you? You're the foreman. They take notice of you. In all that time you didn't say a word.

> RICHARD *hangs his head in shame. There are tears starting to form in his eyes.*

RICHARD: I couldn't've stopped them.
MAUREEN: Did you try? No! Weak. They told him the guys who worked at Dynon's said that the Baldoni's guys were fairies, and he went and took them on and got himself half killed. Big joke.
GLEN: The Dynon's guys did say that, Mum. They did. You're making me sound like an idiot!
MAUREEN: [*to* RICHARD] Yeah, you hang your head in shame. Too late now.

> *There's a pause.* JACK *looks at* RICHARD *and* LUKA.

JACK: You guys want to say anything?

> *There's another pause.*

RICHARD: [*to* GLEN] Sorry mate.
GLEN: You weren't the one got me into fights. Luka and Nookie got me into the fights. And Nookie and Macca borrowed me money, and always said they were giving it back next week. An' they never did.
RICHARD: [*to* GLEN] Sorry mate. I should've stopped it. I'm ashamed of it now, but I used to laugh along with 'em. After a week of putting up scaffolds everyone's lookin' for any laugh they can get. [*Pause.*] No excuse. Sorry mate.

> GLEN *comes across with tears in his eyes and gives* RICHARD *another hug. He goes back to his seat.* JACK *looks at* LUKA.

LUKA: What is this? The fuckin' girl guides? I'm not apologising. I'm not going to start hugging everyone. What is this?

> JACK *looks at* LUKA *steadily.*

You ever worked in a place like ours, mate?
JACK: I've worked in worse, *mate*.
MAUREEN: You won't get him to apologise. He's the bloody ringleader.
LUKA: If you ever worked in a place like Baldoni's you'd know that everyone takes the piss out of everyone all the bloody time. It's the only way to stay sane. You take it and give back as good as you get.
MAUREEN: The only one who was taking it was Glen.
LUKA: Who do you bloody think was taking it before he came along?

> *There's a silence.*

I was. [*He turns on* RICHARD.] How about you apologise to me as well? Hey?
RICHARD: Everyone cops a bit of stick.
LUKA: I been in this country since I was eight. And they call me a fucking killer 'cause my dad's a Serb. 'All your Serb mates are good for is raping women.' That's what they said. [*To* RICHARD] So why don't you apologise to me?
RICHARD: Mate, it wasn't that bad.
LUKA: Oh yeah. Over the bloody loudspeaker system: 'Luka is barred from the lunch room because he eats stinking wog food.' Big joke.
RICHARD: It *was* just a joke.
LUKA: It was you that made the announcement. The bloody foreman. Setting a great example. And when I go to the lunch room they've taken out my chair and it's sitting in the middle of the yard. With a sign on it saying 'Rapists and Killers eat here'.

RICHARD: It was a joke.
LUKA: [to JACK] I eat pies and shit just like the rest of them and they say I eat stinking wog food.
JACK: Why did you make that announcement, Richard?
RICHARD: I didn't think of the idea. Mac and Nookie pressured me to do it 'cause it'd sound more official.
JACK: So why didn't you say no?
LUKA: Yeah, why didn't you say no?!
RICHARD: Shit mate. You've got to fit in. Especially if you're a foreman. Otherwise everyone thinks you're too big for your boots.
LUKA: Does everything they tell him. Does everything anyone tells him. Sold us all out to Greg too.
GREG: No one's been sold out!
LUKA: Worst workplace agreement I've ever seen. No overtime rates, no nothing.
GREG: You all got an increase in your basic rate!
LUKA: Yeah, and it doesn't even begin to cover what we lost in overtime.
RICHARD: I didn't push you all.
LUKA: Not much. 'We don't need the unions here,' he tells us, 'Greg will look after us.' Yeah.
GREG: If you don't like it, just go and work somewhere else, Luka.
LUKA: Yeah, like where?
GREG: I gave you all a ten per cent rise.
LUKA: [to RICHARD] Don't need the bloody unions. Like hell we don't need the bloody unions.
GREG: First time I've known you were unhappy, Luka.
LUKA: Because everyone's too shit scared to say anything.
JACK: Luka. We're not here today to say things that might make it difficult for you at work.
LUKA: You talk about Glen getting a rough time. Sometimes I go home from work and I'm so angry inside I just wanna kill someone.
JACK: Because of the wog food stuff?
LUKA: The whole place. The whole life. The whole stinkin' hopelessness of it all. You say you've worked in a place worse than where we work?
JACK: Yeah.
LUKA: I doubt it, mate. You erect the same bloody scaffolds. Time after time. You take 'em down and put 'em up again somewhere else. It's

the pits, man. For anyone with half a brain it's the pits. We're the dregs. And we know it. And if we don't behave like girl guides—if we do spend all our bloody day giving shit to anyone who'll let it get to them—the reason is that we all know we're the dregs. We're ashamed, mate. We're ashamed of ourselves, and if we can make anyone feel worse than we do, then we feel better. A hell of a lot better.

JACK: I know what you're saying.

LUKA: Where did you work that was so bloody bad?

JACK: Try working in a mine.

LUKA: This job's fine for Glen. Same dreary thing, day in, day out. He doesn't care. Loves it.

MAUREEN: Don't talk about him as if he's stupid.

LUKA: [*erupting*] Let's stop talking shit. Glen, mate, I'm sorry, but you're not real bright.

GLEN: I'm not stupid.

BARRY: You call him stupid one more time, mate, and I'll clock you one right here and now.

GLEN: I jus' get upset. I get confused. I'm not stupid!

LUKA: All I'm saying is that the sad thing is that he's the one going and he loves the job. We all hate it and we stay.

GREG: If you hate it that much then shove off.

LUKA: To where?

JACK: Greg, it won't help things if you start making threats.

GREG: He's sitting there telling us he hates working for me.

JACK: We're trying to be open today. We're trying to say all the things we don't normally say.

GREG: I can't see what bloody good it's doing.

JACK: There's a lot of factors that helped make a wreck of your Mercedes, Greg, and maybe we can sort some of them out.

GLEN: I'm not stupid. I just get confused by things.

MAUREEN: You're fine, son. You're the best son I ever had.

GLEN: I'm the only son you ever had.

MAUREEN: And I wouldn't swap you for anyone. Not even Mel Gibson.

She puts her arm around his shoulder and hugs him.

GLEN: I get confused.

LUKA: [*to* JACK] Miners get well paid. At least they get well paid. We're the bottom of the barrel. We're the shit of the earth and we know it.

I go home and watch television in my one-bedroom bloody hovel and there's these American shows with rich guys making jokes about their wives. They should be so bloody lucky. To *have* a wife. No woman would ever look at the likes of me. We're just shit. Greg gets all upset because his Mercedes gets dented. Big deal. Lose your no claim bonus. Big deal.

GREG: I had my neck in a brace for weeks.

LUKA: I got my life in a brace. For good.

GREG: Car wrecked in your own driveway. Shouted at. Threatened.

LUKA: Maybe someone *should* shout at you. You pay the worst rates in the whole industry.

GREG: Go and work somewhere else.

LUKA: Yeah, where? Waiting lists a mile long. Only get a job if your father had it. People are queuing up for shit jobs in this country and they make fun of where my father came from!

GREG: I've got a mate setting up a business in China, Luka, and there are millions upon millions there who'd be happy to do what you do for a dollar and two bowls of rice a day.

LUKA: I'm not in bloody China.

GREG: Why should you be getting fifty times as much for the same work? This is an international bloody economy. Why should a union be giving you guys special protection?

CLAIRE: Greg, don't get upset.

GREG: The pricks don't know when they're well off! Because of what I started twenty-seven years ago, seventy-two employees go home with a wage *fifty* times what they'd get in China, and all I get is whinges.

LUKA: I don't give a shit what they pay in China. All I know is that here in Australia I get two dollars an hour less than guys doing exactly the same as me!

GREG: It *is* a bloody tragedy that Glen's got to go. He works harder than the next two of you put together.

GLEN: I'll work even harder, Mr Baldoni. I promise.

There's a silence.

I'll pay for your car. I'll work it off.

There's another silence.

FACE TO FACE

RICHARD: [*to* LUKA] I don't know where you get this figure of two dollars an hour, mate.

LUKA: [*angrily*] We're two dollars an hour lower than anyone else in the industry, and you told us all we should take it!

GREG: As I keep telling you, Luka. You don't have to work for me.

JACK: Isn't it better you know how your workforce feels, Greg?

LUKA: He'll sack me for speaking out for sure, but I don't bloody care anymore. I came along here today to speak my mind and I'm gonna. I'd be almost as well off on the dole in any case. It's time to say something and I'm bloody going to say it.

JACK: Are you paying the lowest rates in the industry, Greg?

GREG: We're not here today to talk about what I pay or don't pay. I came out of respect for Maureen. For her sake I don't want Glen to go to prison. It's not me who's on trial here today, and if you start treating me like I am, I'm out of here, and Glen can take his chances.

JACK: Would you like your firm to work better and be more profitable, Greg?

From left: Barry Langrishe as Greg, Sharon Flanigan as Claire and Andrew Doyle as Luka in the 1999 Ensemble Theatre production in Sydney. (Photo: Geoff Beatty)

GREG: Sure, but what the hell has that got to do with me being assaulted in my driveway?

JACK: Maybe quite a lot. I'd like to hear a bit more about the morale in your firm, Greg. Can we pursue this a little further?

CLAIRE: Greg knows damn well that things aren't good at work.

GREG: Claire, just keep out of this.

CLAIRE: Greg, you complain to me all the time that the firm's not running like it should be running. How you're starting to miss out on contracts, because the work's never done on time these days, and it's slipshod, and there's too much absenteeism, and too many accidents. I hear it night after night.

GREG: This is not the place to tackle workplace issues.

CLAIRE: You didn't tell me you're paying them less than the other firms.

GREG: I pay what I can afford to pay. We're just this side of solvent. Right Therese?

THERESE: It's pretty tight.

LUKA: So I guess you won't be spending two months in Italy and France this year?

JACK: Luka.

LUKA: And you'll be selling your yacht?

GREG: Luka, if you had the intelligence and gumption to risk everything and start a business and work at it for twenty-seven years, then maybe you'd feel entitled to a few rewards.

JACK: Luka, we've heard enough from you for a while, mate.

RICHARD: Our rates might be a bit lower than the rest, but I don't think it's anywhere near two dollars an hour.

LUKA: You wouldn't. You were the one who sold us out. Told us we didn't need the union.

GREG: Unions are a thing of the past.

LUKA: Who else is going to protect us from people like you?

GREG: The market protects you. If you've got skills and I don't pay you enough for them, you go somewhere else.

LUKA: I got skills. I'm a trained fitter and turner. But suddenly we've got no manufacturing industry anymore. Because companies can go to China and pay one dollar a day and two bowls of rice.

RICHARD: Name me one place that's paying—

LUKA: Dynon's for a start. You know what you did to us and we know why!

RICHARD: What was the union ever going to do for us, eh? Take their fat salaries and tell us to go on strike. We got an okay deal.
LUKA: We got a shit deal and you told us to take it because Greg promised you the manager's job. Huh?
RICHARD: That's shit, Luka!
LUKA: We know.
RICHARD: That's shit.
LUKA: Greg promised you the manager's job. Then he doublecrossed you and gave it to Adrian, and we've all been done.
GREG: I never promised anything.
LUKA: You promised him the manager's job.
GREG: What would you know?
LUKA: Plenty. Richard told Davo when he was drunk one night. 'I'm outta this,' he told Davo. 'Office job coming up.' [*To* RICHARD] Except you didn't get it, did ya? Our owner gives it to his bloody son.
GREG: I never promised Richard anything. I said it *might* happen.
RICHARD: You said I had it.
GREG: You're turning on me too?
RICHARD: You did promise, mate.
GREG: And I meant it. But family comes first.
LUKA: [*to* RICHARD] What a sucker you were.
GREG: Look, this is *my* business. I built it. I own it. Adrian was stuffing up his life. I had to find something for him.
RICHARD: Yeah.
GREG: You've got kids. You know how it is.
RICHARD: Yeah.
CLAIRE: [*to* RICHARD] Greg is perfectly entitled to give his own son a job. This is ridiculous. [*To* GREG] Adrian wasn't 'stuffing' up his life, Greg. He just got in with the wrong crowd at university.
LUKA: And he's still smoking the stuff non-stop in case you haven't noticed.
JACK: Luka.
LUKA: I don't give a shit, Jack. He can sack me. I don't give a shit. I can finally say what I feel. Nobody *ever* says what they feel at Baldoni's. All that happens is that everyone takes the piss out of each other, day in, day out. No one says anything that's real. Ever! Well, I'm saying things that are real and I'm not going to stop. What happens at Baldoni's is sick. It's sick and it makes me sick and I'm gonna say it!

JACK: Thanks Luka. I think all of us are pretty clear about how you feel.
GREG: Look I'm sorry, but erecting scaffolds is never going to be the work they do in heaven!
JACK: Could things still be a little better than they are?
GREG: Don't try and tell me Luka's got the answers.
LUKA: I know a hell of a lot more than you about what's goin' on.
GREG: Such as?
LUKA: Your son hates the place. An' I'm not saying that to get you upset. I like your kid. But he's not cut out for it and he's not happy.
GREG: How would you know?
LUKA: Because I talk to him. Do you?
GREG: I've really had enough of you, Luka.
JACK: [*to* GREG] Maybe he's telling you something you should know.
CLAIRE: We know he's not happy, but we're doing our best and he's doing his best.
GREG: He's not still smoking dope. That's bullshit.
RICHARD: He is, Greg. All the time.
LUKA: Why wouldn't he be?
GREG: What's that meant to mean?
LUKA: I just feel sorry for that kid.
GREG: Why? Because he's got parents who do everything they can for him?
LUKA: Forget it.
GREG: He's doing okay.
LUKA: He's not doing okay. When you keep hearing shit about your old man day after day, how can you be doing okay?
CLAIRE: What's he hearing?
RICHARD: They tell him stuff to upset him.
GREG: Lies.
CLAIRE: What kind of lies?
RICHARD: That his dad pays himself too much and takes too many holidays. That sort of stuff.
LUKA: He hears more than that.
CLAIRE: What?
GREG: Rumours, lies. They make it up.
JACK: Luka, is this important?
LUKA: No. Sorry. [*Looking at* CLAIRE] Forget it.

CLAIRE *picks up the glance and is suddenly alerted. She looks at* GREG.

CLAIRE: Not again, Greg.
GREG: Again, what?
CLAIRE: I wondered why Adrian's been so—kind to me lately.
GREG: What are you talking about?
CLAIRE: All those interstate trips! For God's sake, you hardly do any business interstate. I must be an idiot!
GREG: There is nothing going on!
CLAIRE: And Julie just happens to go with you every time!
GREG: She's my personal assistant, for God's sake. She has to come.
JULIE: There's nothing going on, Claire. I swear to you.
JACK: Is this a path we want to go down?
CLAIRE: Yes!
JULIE: Claire, there is absolutely nothing going on. I swear.
JACK: Good, now can we—?
CLAIRE: Was there once?
JULIE: It doesn't matter. I've handed in my resignation. I'm going.
GREG: This is lovely. In front of my employees.
LUKA: We know already.
JACK: Are we sure this is a path—?
CLAIRE: [*to* GREG] What is it with you? Have you got a cog missing in your brain or something?
JULIE: I'm really sorry, Claire.
CLAIRE: It's not your fault. If you say no, he can fire you.
JULIE: No, it was mainly my fault.
CLAIRE: I bet. It wasn't until you stripped naked and did an arabesque that he took any notice whatsoever. Come on! This isn't the first time he's done it, as someone else who's here today could soon tell you.
MAUREEN: Claire!
CLAIRE: I'm not trying to get at you, Maureen. I'm just fed up with him!

She moves away from her husband. GLEN *frowns.*

GLEN: [*to* MAUREEN] Were you and Mr Baldoni—?
MAUREEN: No! Well, not for long.
JACK: Are we sure this is a fruitful path?
CLAIRE: Very fruitful!

JULIE: Truly, it was more my fault than his, and I feel really ashamed.
CLAIRE: Don't try and make me feel better.
JULIE: It's true. I made the moves.
CLAIRE: You couldn't be that desperate!
GREG: Thank you!
CLAIRE: You're not exactly God's gift to women.
GREG: I'm going.
CLAIRE: Just you sit there.

  GREG *gets up to leave.*

JACK: Greg, if you walk out now Glen'll probably go to prison.
GREG: I couldn't give a shit.
JACK: Yeah well, mate, I could. Because if he does, what'll happen to him won't be pretty.
GLEN: I'm not going to prison. No way. I'll kill m'self first.
MAUREEN: Greg. Stay. Please, for my sake.
GREG: I gave your kid a job and look what it's done for me!
MAUREEN: Please Greg. Stay.
CLAIRE: You just sit there, Greg. You owe her that much.
GREG: What do I owe her?! We only made it to bed three times before you twigged and worked me over.
GLEN: [*to* MAUREEN] Is that why Dad shot himself?
MAUREEN: No! Glen, it was after that.
GLEN: [*glowering at* GREG] Should have rammed him sooner!
GREG: That's it. I'm out of here.
JACK: Greg. If someone like Glen goes to prison it's the end for them. I've seen it happen.
GLEN: What d'you mean? Someone like me? What am I? A freak or somethin'?!
JACK: Mate, you like people, you trust people and you're not rat cunning. They'll turn you into a crazed bloody animal. [*To* GREG] Do you want that on your conscience?
BARRY: [*to* GREG] You fucking leave, mate, an' we'll *really* do a job on your Mercedes!
JACK: BARRY!
GLEN: I'm not goin' t'prison, I'm goin' back to work! For fuck's sake, why d'you think I'm here today? I wanna get back to work!
BARRY: Mate, it's goin' to be all right.

JACK: Greg, just stay and I'll get this back on track. I promise.
GREG: I'm not staying if his mate's going to threaten me and she's [*indicating* CLAIRE] going to be sitting there insulting me the rest of the afternoon.
CLAIRE: For God's sake. I've just found out you've been having an affair with someone half your age! Don't you think I'm going to be a *little* bit angry!
JULIE: Claire, it really was more my fault than his.
CLAIRE: Oh, yes. Once you were in the force-field of his animal magnetism, you just couldn't help yourself.
JULIE: Actually it was far more mundane than that.

There's a silence. They all look at her.

[*To* CLAIRE] I dragged myself out of bed one morning and thought about yet another wildly interesting day writing letters to idiots about clamps and tubes and formwork and erection schedules, and thought, 'No! Anything has to be better than this.' [*Pause.*] I'd just spent two days organising the itinerary for your eight weeks in Tuscany and Provence. I'd picked the charming cottages and the fabulous restaurants and suddenly I found myself with tears of anger rolling down my cheeks saying, 'Why not me?!'
GREG: Deep down I knew that was it.
JULIE: Claire, I'm not a brilliant PA. If I was, I wouldn't be working for your husband. I'd be in some merchant banker's world headquarters meeting young unmarried international business hotshots. But the truth is I'm pretty average. Frankly, the only reason I get work is the way I look, and that's not going to last forever.

She sighs again.

CLAIRE: So what went wrong?
GREG: I knew what she was after. I just wouldn't be in it.
JULIE: I thought of you, believe it or not. I thought that anyone who can put up with nearly thirty years of Greg has earned Tuscany and Provence.
GREG: I knew what you were after and I had no intention of leaving Claire.
JULIE: Well, if you didn't you were a good liar. Claire, I'm sorry. I'm really sorry. I'd better go.

JACK: Julie, the main agenda today is what happens to Glen. I'd really appreciate it if you could stay too.
JULIE: It was stupid right from the start. Claire, I really am sorry.

She bursts into tears and CLAIRE *moves across and hugs her.*

LUKA: [*to* JACK] Jesus, is there normally so much friggin' hugging and shit?
JACK: Yeah, a bit of hugging is pretty normal.
CLAIRE: I hope he gave you a bit more excitement than he's ever given me.
JULIE: I'm sorry. I should go.
CLAIRE: Please. Stay.
GREG: She made the moves!
CLAIRE: And you resisted with all your might. [*To* MAUREEN] Sorry, Maureen, I didn't mean to bring you into this.
MAUREEN: I should've apologised to you too.

She moves across and hugs CLAIRE.

LUKA: Let's all just hug each other and get it bloody over with.
MAUREEN: I should've apologised years ago. I swear to you I wasn't after Tuscany. Spaghetti and meatballs is my limit.
CLAIRE: It wasn't your fault.
MAUREEN: Well, it was a bit. It was flattering to have some bloke who wasn't a total deadbeat pay me some attention.
GREG: I'm glad I'm not a *total* deadbeat.
MAUREEN: You're better than most.
GREG: Someone said something nice about me? Am I dreaming?
JACK: Anyone else had an affair they'd like to talk about? Good. Maybe we can limp back to the main agenda.
GLEN: Is that why you had to stop workin' for him, Mum? 'Cause Mrs Baldoni found out?
MAUREEN: Yes.
GLEN: [*to* GREG] She was out of a job for months.
GREG: I know, Glen. I did my best to help. [*He looks at his wife and two ex-lovers.*] Do you all have to sit together?
JACK: Richard. You're the foreman. Tell us about the workplace. Earlier Claire suggested that— [*Reading the notes he's taken*] 'The work's never done on time these days, it's slipshod, there's too much absenteeism, and too many accidents.' Sounds like something's wrong?

LUKA: We're doing as little as we can get away with because you're paying us as little as you can get away with.

RICHARD: I shouldn't've sold them what you were offering, Greg.

LUKA: [*to* GREG, *pointing to* RICHARD] We respected this guy. Straightest guy we'd ever worked for. He came and told us he'd looked over the books and it was all you could afford, and we believed him.

GREG: It was true.

RICHARD: I never even looked at the books. The truth is I *was* desperate to get that office job. The sheer heaven of sitting on your bum all day. The sheer heaven of not having to disguise an order as a request. The sheer heaven of not having to stay 'mates' with some of the biggest pricks you'd ever met in your life.

LUKA: Thanks.

RICHARD: Nookie and Mac! Sit there and watch them steal off Glen every payday and not even be able to say a word.

LUKA: You should've.

RICHARD: Did you ever say anything?

LUKA: I would've if I was bloody foreman.

JACK: Do you think you *did* sell your mates out, Richard?

RICHARD: 'Course I did.

JACK: So how does that make you feel?

RICHARD: How do you think it makes me bloody feel? Nookie and Mac I'd sell out any day of the week, but the rest, by and large are decent guys doing the best they can in a job that can drive a bloke crazy. I'll apologise to everyone tomorrow.

LUKA: That's going to do a fat lot of good.

RICHARD: [*with sudden anger*] Greg, if you want to do something about the morale round the place then for fuck's sake pay the going rate.

GREG: I can't! Therese, tell 'em how close to the edge we are.

    THERESE *hesitates.*

Tell 'em. Let 'em all hear the facts.

THERESE: Our operating profit is quite slim.

GREG: Tell 'em last year's profit.

THERESE: A couple of thousand dollars.

GREG: A couple of thousand dollars. On a turnover of millions. That's how close to the wind we are.

JACK: Would you be willing to tell us a little more about your cost structure? Materials, wages, management package?

LUKA: How much do you pay yourself a year, Greg?
GREG: That's my business.
JACK: When I rang around I did pick up a lot of anger about the amount you're paying yourself, Greg.
GREG: I get what any CEO in a firm with this sort of turnover would get.
JACK: Is that right, Therese?
GREG: You've got no right to ask her that.
JACK: If you feel it puts you in a difficult position, Therese, of course you don't have to answer.

He looks steadily at THERESE. *There's a silence.*

THERESE: Greg pays himself twice as much as he should in my opinion.
GREG: Therese!
THERESE: It's made me angry for a long while. Not just the salary. The perks. The travel. It's just made me so angry. I have to break the law to get the accounts through the auditor.
GREG: That's bullshit, Therese!
THERESE: I have to break the law and I hate it.
GREG: That's a lie.
THERESE: I've been applying for other jobs for years. I would have got out years ago but I'm hopeless at interviews.
GREG: Therese, everyone interprets the law to their own advantage.
THERESE: [*with sudden anger, to* JULIE] You're very sorry now. [*To* JACK] Conference in Brisbane? Like hell. They were both on Hayman Island for a week! And I had to fudge it all. Conference in Adelaide. Like hell. Trip round the Barossa in the best hotels. It went on and on. [*To* JULIE] I'm 'off-putting', am I? Okay, I don't go out drinking, flirting, chatting away about *nothing* like you do. Pushing myself forward as if I was God's gift to the universe like you do. Okay, but I also don't go cheating on someone as decent as Claire. I don't go ripping off the firm for thousands and thousands of dollars to sleep with the boss on luxury holidays. Dollars that could've gone to the men out there who actually work. And if I did do it and was caught out I'd be sensitive enough to realise I couldn't just expect to shrug it all off with a few tears and hugs!
JACK: Hang on, Therese. Is this really helpful?
THERESE: It is to me! [*To* JULIE] Crocodile tears. In a week or two you'll be out finding some other victim to get your hooks into.

JULIE: Finished?

JACK: I hope so.

JULIE: [*to* THERESE] Had your little hate spasm? Make you feel good? Just for your information I won't ever be getting involved with a married man again. Which will probably doom me to a very long relationship with my word processor, because the few men that you'd want to marry out there find commitment about as inviting as swallowing snot. Yes I had a few holidays. A bit of sun. A few very good meals. One bottle of Grange Hermitage. First ever and last ever. You know what I'd rather have? Pathetic as it may sound, a good husband and some kids. Some chance.

    THERESE *hangs her head.*

[*To* THERESE] Sorry. Sorry. I'm just doing everything wrong today.

JACK: I'm not sure you are.

JULIE: You married?

JACK: Yeah, four kids. My brother's just divorced though.

JULIE: Is he like you?

JACK: No, he's a pig.

JULIE: Story of my life.

JACK: Greg. You're paying yourself too much, mate. That's what your accountant reckons. You'd do better if you gave a bit more to the guys that are doing it for you out there. How do you feel about that?

THERESE: If we could claw back the market share we've lost, the extra wages would more than pay for themselves.

JACK: There's your accountant speaking, Greg. What do you reckon?

GREG: Fine in theory, but how much would it really solve? Give them two dollars an hour more and they're going to flog their guts out for me? Dream on.

RICHARD: No, they're never going to flog their guts out for you, Greg.

GREG: See?

RICHARD: Eight weeks in Europe? Italian cooking lessons? They're not going to flog their guts out for you ever, mate. But pay 'em what they should be paid and at least they wouldn't sabotage you.

LUKA: [*to* GREG] Like I said, mate. From where I stand anyone with a wife like your wife is bloody lucky, and all you do is cheat on her. So you're not my favourite person. But shit, mate, pay us fair and at least the hate level will go down a little. At least we won't actively fucking sabotage you.

CLAIRE: You waste your money on idiotic things in any case, Greg.
GREG: Like what?
CLAIRE: That stupid yacht. All you do with it is sail it down to Tasmania once a year, and get sick as a dog and come near enough to last. You're trying to compete against *real* money and they laugh.
GREG: Nobody laughs!
CLAIRE: Yes they do. And then you rage around the house for a week. You're not the big league, Greg, and it's about time you realised!
GREG: I employ seventy-six people.
CLAIRE: Move aside Bill Gates.
GREG: I'm not trying to be Bill Gates!
JACK: You don't have to be, mate. He's a nerd.
CLAIRE: We don't *both* need a top-of-the-range Mercedes. We don't need a huge holiday house we go to once a year. We don't need to drink such expensive wine. And we *certainly* don't need that stupid yacht.
JACK: Does your accountant have a view on the yacht?
LUKA: Tell us where it's moored and I'll sink the bloody thing.
THERESE: If Greg just took a normal CEO package we could afford a more generous wage structure.
JACK: A consensus seems to be emerging, Greg.
GREG: [*to* JACK] Who do you think you are, mate? A bloody management consultant?
JACK: If I was I'd be charging a hell of lot more, and telling you nothing of any use whatsoever. So, Therese, you're telling us that if Greg drank cheaper wines, and stopped heaving his lunch into the sea, an extra two dollars an hour is totally feasible?
THERESE: Absolutely.
LUKA: And if you combined that with letting us in on what the hell is going on round the place, then we might really be getting somewhere.
GREG: What's going on?
LUKA: How the firm is travelling. Whether the work is coming in. Whether we're gonna try a new computer scheduling system like Dynon's. At the moment there's no bloody communication of any sort. It's just like we don't bloody exist.
GREG: Does anybody *want* to hear that sort of stuff?
LUKA: I do for sure. I might feel like I was actually part of the place. And I might say one or two good things about it when I was drinking in the pub, instead of bitching and badmouthing it like everyone else.

CLAIRE: Greg, it makes sense.
GREG: [*to* LUKA] Are you telling me that deadheads like Mac and Nookie are going to be interested in that sort of stuff?
LUKA: Mac and Nookie are barely interested enough in the world to keep breathin'.
RICHARD: If those two went, a lot of our problems would disappear overnight.
THERESE: And if you sent Adrian back to finish his uni course—
GREG: He hated it.
THERESE: After six months working for us I think you'll find he sees it in a more positive light.
GREG: Why hasn't he told *me* that?
LUKA: He doesn't want you to think he can't hack it.
CLAIRE: [*to* GREG] He hinted to me that he was reconsidering things, just a few days ago.
GREG: [*sarcastically*] Anything else I should do?
JULIE: In my opinion, which isn't of course worth much because I'm only the company harlot, you should give Richard the job you promised him, make Luka foreman.
GREG: Anything else?
JULIE: [*nodding*] You should give Glen a good redundancy package too.
GREG: Glen? He smashed my Mercedes? Gave me whiplash.
THERESE: [*to* GREG] It wasn't his fault. They've been picking on him ever since he came.
JULIE: He worked twice as hard as most of them. It's wrong to just sack him.
GLEN: I don' *want* a package. I want my job.
GREG: [*to* THERESE *and* JULIE] Maybe I should just stay home and let you two run the place.
CLAIRE: They're talking sense. Just listen for a change, will you Greg?
THERESE: Sorry Mr Baldoni. I didn't mean to say all these things, but it's what I've been thinking for a long while.
GLEN: [*to* JACK] I don' want a package. I want my job.
JACK: I don't know that that's going to be possible, Glen.
GLEN: That job was me bloody life! They all say how they hate it, well I don'. You start wif nothin' and every time when you finish, it's like—it's like—you really done somethin'. People come and see the exhibitions and all the things that're on the stands and you come

and look at them looking and you know inside you done it all. Everything they're lookin' at is there because you made the stands. That job's me bloody life.

There's a silence. GLEN *has his head down with tears in his eyes.*

That job's me bloody life.

BARRY: Jesus, give the guy a fucking break, will you? You're all carrying on about your own little problems, and this guy is dying in front of you. Do you know anything about him? Do you know what he and his mum went through? Any of you know about his old man? Jack, I just want a few minutes to talk about what these two've been through.

JACK: Go for it.

BARRY: When I first met this guy he used to come to school with black eyes and bruises. Any of you ever met his dad?

There's a silence.

Well, you're lucky. Fucking pig. My old man was a drunk and you could understand it a bit more when he lost it, but Stan never had more than a few beers. Lost it when he was sober. Maureen didn't measure up and Glen certainly didn't. Every time he made a mistake at anything he got bashed, and Maureen—

MAUREEN: I didn't get bashed, Barry.

BARRY: No, you didn't get bashed but you got shouted out, day in day out. I heard it, Mrs Tregaskis.

MAUREEN: He was hard on Glen. Used to make me cry the way he treated him and nothing I said made any difference.

GLEN: Called me 'Thick'. Not jus' like 'Hey, Glen, you're thick.' He *called* me 'Thick'. 'Thick, get out and mow the lawn.' 'Thick, get in and clean your room.' Never remember him *ever* calling me Glen.

BARRY: 'Course we didn't help at school. You know what little pricks you are at that age. We all called him 'Thick' too.

GLEN: Mum was the only one that called me me bloody name.

MAUREEN: He used to cry in the morning and plead with me not to send him to school. It was a total humiliation for him in every way.

BARRY: One day I just pushed it too far and he let out a scream and went for me. He was only little in those days too, and I was a big prick, but he did me over totally. Nearly fucking killed me. Sorry Mrs Tregaskis. Shouldn't swear. That's when we became mates. I thought to m'self this guy hurts. This guy is human. I'm a bit of a prick but I'm not an animal and this guy was hurting.

GLEN: If Barry caught anyone calling me 'Thick' he bashed the shit outta them. Sorry Mum. Barry's always been me best mate. Stopped me from killin' Dad.

There's a silence.

Duncan Young (left) as Glen and Amos Szeps as Barry in the 1999 Ensemble Theatre production in Sydney. (Photo: Geoff Beatty)

BARRY: You weren't gonna kill him, mate.

GLEN: Fuckin' oath I was.

BARRY: No mate. You were just gonna give him a scare.

GLEN: No, I was gonna fucking kill him. I'd had enough, mate.

BARRY: Mate, you've just got it wrong in your mind.

GLEN: Mate, if I had've got to him, he was dead.

JACK: Barry?

MAUREEN: Stan used to let Glen back up and down the drive in the car if he washed it properly, and he scraped it on the garage door.

GLEN: Acciden'al. It was acciden'al.

MAUREEN: Glen was only fifteen and not big like he is now and Stan was huge. I screamed at Stan to stop hitting him, but by the time he did, Glen was a mess. Stan went off to his club and next thing I know I see Glen heading off with Stan's shotgun. I panicked and rang Barry.

BARRY: I shot off and grabbed the gun off him before he got there.

GLEN: I woulda killed him, Barry. I fuckin' woulda killed him.

MAUREEN: We hid the gun under some boxes at the back of the shed. Luckily Stan never looked for it.

JACK: [*to* GLEN] You finally had it out with your Dad, didn't you?

GLEN: One day he shouted at Mum so bad I jus' lost it.

MAUREEN: Round about sixteen or seventeen Glen grew and filled out. Suddenly his father met his match. I tell you what. I shouldn't've but I bloody cheered.

GLEN: [*excitedly*] I give it to him, didn' I, Mum?

MAUREEN: I cheered. He couldn't take it. Couldn't take the humiliation. Big strong Stan. Man's man. Tough as nails. Thrashed by his own son.

GLEN: [*excitedly, acting it out*] He was down on the floor bleedin' from the nose, an' I shouted, 'Get up an call me "Thick". Go on, get up and call me "Thick" and see what happens to ya.' Never did. Too fuckin' scared. Big fuckin' Stan the man. Scared of his own little kid. Sorry Mum.

MAUREEN: He couldn't take the humiliation. Packed his bags and left that day.

GLEN: Went and stayed with his mum. Only one who could stand him. Stan the fuckin' man. Bought another gun and said he was gonna come and kill us both.

MAUREEN: He meant it.

GLEN: I wasn' scared. Only for Mum.

MAUREEN: When we saw him parked outside at four in the morning with a gun in his hand we got to hell out of there. That's why we ended up here.

GLEN: Didn't shoot us. Shot 'is bloody self. I wasn' even gonna go to his fuckin' funeral but Mum made me.

BARRY: [*to* GREG] Glen's had it tougher than any of us ever did. If he's a bit touchy you can see why. Me and some of his other mates will kick in and help him pay off your no claim bonus, Mr Baldoni. If you get rid of those two troublemakers he won't give you any more shit. Will you Glen, mate?

GLEN: No way, Barry.

JACK: We've got a few more ends to tie up before we can start asking Greg to make that sort of decision.

BARRY: Youse've all heard what he's been through?

JACK: Yes, we have, thank you very much, Barry, but—

BARRY: Anyone who's been through that sorta shit's gonna be touchy.

JACK: Yep.

BARRY: So what's the problem?

JACK: Barry seems to think there's no problem.

LUKA: 'Course there's a problem. I don't care what caused it. The fact is that when Glen loses it he's bloody dangerous!

JACK: Barry?

BARRY: He's got a temper. You just gotta learn how to handle him.

JACK: Have you always been able to handle him, Barry?

> JACK *looks steadily at* BARRY. BARRY *frowns at* GLEN.

BARRY: Glen, you didn't tell him about… oh shit!

GLEN: He tol' me to tell the truth about all the times in the past I'd lost it.

BARRY: [*despairing*] Glen…

GLEN: He said, 'You gotta trust me.' And I trust him.

BARRY: Well, you shouldn't've, mate. He's not on your side. He just sits in the centre.

GLEN: I trust him.

JACK: Would you like to tell us about it, Barry?

BARRY: Wouldn't happen now.

JACK *keeps his eyes steadily on* BARRY.

Me an' me mates aren't saints. Glen's great fun most of the time but he can get on your nerves sometimes. [*To* GLEN] Sorry, mate, but everyone's spillin' their guts— [*To* JACK] He can keep on and on on the same note and he was drivin' us mad about women.

LUKA: Don't we know it, mate.

BARRY: This girl was givin' him the eye. That girl was givin' him the eye. Every girl in the fuckin' world was givin' him the eye.

GLEN: I was makin' a lot of it up, mate.

BARRY: We *know* you were makin' a lot of it up, mate. That was the bloody problem.

GLEN: You guys all had birds. I didn' want you to think I couldn' get one too.

BARRY: Mate, we did guess that that was the motive, but the fact was we were goin' mad. So we said that if he didn't get a girl soon we'd all go round the bend. So we set him up with this girl to go to the movies with him. She didn't even do it with him.

GLEN: [*angrily*] Yes, she did!

BARRY: Well whatever. She wanted out, and we had to tell him it was a set-up.

GLEN: Bastards!

JACK: Then what happened?

BARRY: He got mad at me.

JACK: A bit more than that, mate.

GLEN: I got me dad's gun.

BARRY: Glen! Mate. [*To* JACK] He's got a temper. We all know that.

JACK: You had to get an AVO out on him, didn't you?

BARRY: For a day or two, until he calmed down. Shit, I'd just had a young baby and Tess was terrified.

LUKA: What's an AVO?

JACK: Apprehended Violence Order.

BARRY: It was only for a few days, then we talked it out an' he was fine.

GLEN: I wasn' 'fine'. I was still shitty, I jus' wasn' gonna kill ya anymore.

JACK: Which must have been a relief, Barry.

BARRY: You didn' need to bring that up.

JACK: I think maybe I did. Before you start telling Greg he should have Glen back, we should know all the facts.

BARRY: When Glen says he loves that job, mate, he's tellin' the truth. Talks about it all the time. 'Built these stands for the motor show.' All the cars were up on *his* stands. Luka, do any of the rest of you go off and see the car show *ten* times so you can look at your stands?

LUKA: Mate, I have nightmares about scaffolding. I wouldn't go *near* any place I'd worked on.

BARRY: See. Have a heart, all of youse.

GLEN: Thanks mate.

BARRY: Have a bloody heart.

JACK: We've all got hearts and they're all bloody, Barry. We've also got heads, and Glen's tendency to explode, whatever the reasons, is a problem. It's a problem we've come here today to deal with and it's a problem we just can't pretend isn't there. I'd like to backtrack a little bit. There's a few things haven't happened yet that I think should happen. There's a few things that have come out that're still worrying me. Therese, are you okay now about what happened to you? You sound as though you were pretty shaken up.

THERESE: I just got panicky. He was in my car and telling me I had to drive off.

GLEN: They tol' me you were jus' shy. I'm sorry. I really am sorry. You were always the nicest person to me in that whole bloody place. I'm sorry.

JACK: You *are* sorry, aren't you, Glen?

GLEN: [*nodding vigorously*] Yeah. Yeah. I feel like givin' her a hug only she'd get scared again.

LUKA: No more bloody hugs.

JACK: Maybe there are some other people around here who are sorry?

He looks at LUKA. LUKA *stares at the floor, but says nothing.* JACK *turns his attention to* RICHARD.

Richard. You regard yourself as a fair and reasonable guy?

CLAIRE: He is.

JACK: That's what I thought. But there was something that came out today that I found really shocking. And I'm not easily shocked. Luka has been here since he was eight, was it?

LUKA: Eight.

JACK: He speaks like an Australian, he thinks like an Australian, he is an Australian. Right Richard? Could you tell us again what was written on that chair in the yard?

RICHARD: We've been through that.

JACK: [*consulting his notes*] Luka said it read 'Rapists and Killers sit here'. Is that right, Richard?

RICHARD: We've been through that.

JACK: I'm not sure. We've been through the fact that the work is hard, boring and monotonous— [*turning to* GLEN] to people who don't get the same kick out of the end result that you do, Glen. We've been through the fact that you feel you're underpaid and unappreciated. We've been through the fact that this gives rise to 'taking the piss' as the only form of amusement. Yeah, we've been through all that. But does all that really excuse this little 'joke'?

RICHARD: I told you! Nookie and Mac would've given me hell if I'd tried to stop them.

JACK: Should Nookie and Mac be having so much influence over everything?

LUKA: Arseholes. They didn't even bother to come here.

GLEN: They'd never come. I phoned Nookie and he said he weren't gonna spill 'is guts in front of a fairy like you. [*Hastily*] I don't think you're a fairy, mate. It's jus' what Nookie said.

JACK: I've only spoken a few words to him over the phone so he must be pretty quick to jump to conclusions, Glen.

GLEN: He and Mac reckon anyone who doesn' work like we do is a fairy.

JACK: They've got a very sophisticated map of the world in their head, haven't they? Sorry. Richard, are they really all that fearsome?

RICHARD: They're a pair of vicious pricks! Jesus, Luka isn't the only one who's copped it from them. I have. They've made *my* life a misery for years.

GLEN: They call him Candle Bum Boy.

JACK: [*to* RICHARD] Please explain?

RICHARD: I've got four kids and things have always been a bit tight financially. Marg makes perfumed candles and stuff like that and we took out a stall at the Paddo Market to sell 'em and earn a few bob. Of course those two found out.

He hangs his head. JACK *waits.*

Yeah, I should've stood up to them. But it's easier said than done. [*He hangs his head again.*] Yeah, I should've stood up to them.

There's another silence. He turns to LUKA.

It was bloody terrible what we did to you, mate. Bloody terrible. And it just went on and on. Sorry.

LUKA: That's okay, mate. I know what pressure you were under.

RICHARD: I wanted to hit 'em a dozen times at least, but I never had the guts. Bloody weak. Sorry.

LUKA: Thanks mate. Really appreciate it.

RICHARD: And I should've stopped what was going on with young Glen too.

LUKA: No mate. That was my fault.

There's a silence. LUKA *looks across at* GLEN.

Mate, it was a joke. I never meant it to lose you your job.

There's another silence.

I was an arsehole. Of all the guys working there you never harmed anyone. I was a total arsehole. Sorry mate. Really sorry.

GLEN, *tears in his eyes, gets up and moves towards* LUKA.

Shit, no hugs mate.

GLEN *and* LUKA *shake hands with genuine enthusiasm.*

GLEN: Let's have a beer.

JACK: No mate, not yet. Haven't quite finished, have we?

Another silence. GLEN *looks at* GREG.

Do you understand now why you were sacked, Glen?

GLEN: I beat up Richard.

JACK: And Richard wasn't even the one who hurt you, was he?

GLEN: [*after a pause*] No.

JACK: And you hurt Richard really badly, didn't you?

GLEN: Yeah.

JACK: So what did Greg have to do?

GLEN: Sack me.

JACK: So was it Greg's fault?

GLEN: No. It was Luka's fault.

JACK: And Luka's just said he's sorry.

There's a pause.

Glen, sometimes you make out you can't understand things when you bloody well can, and I'm getting fed up with it.

BARRY: Fair go, mate!
JACK: Yeah. Every time he does his dumb act, mate, Barry is there to protect him. Well, that might make you feel good, Barry, but it doesn't help Glen. Believe me.
GLEN: I'm not gonna say sorry to him! [*Pointing to* GREG] He gave Mum the sack too, and she was crying for weeks and couldn' get another job.
JACK: Now you know the reason why she was crying, Glen. Come on. Make an effort!
GLEN: [*indicating* GREG] He's a shit.
JACK: Is he, Maureen?
MAUREEN: Glen, when you couldn't get a job and I was desperate, I phoned Greg and he put you on the payroll without a second's hesitation.

There's a silence.

JACK: No one's going to force you to do anything, Glen. It's your call. But just remember the people here today who have put their pride on the line to say sorry to you. Maybe you're not Einstein, but you're not stupid either. Or are you? Are you really 'thick', Glen? Do you want to hide behind what your father did to you all your life?
BARRY: Steady on, mate!
JACK: Just shut up, Barry. For once this is his call.
GLEN: What am I supposed to do?
JACK: [*angrily*] You're supposed to say sorry for wrecking a man's car, for putting his life at risk, and for thinking that you were totally entitled to do it. But if you don't want to do it, let's just forget this whole bloody thing.

There's a silence.

There's nowhere to hide, mate. Either you can control your temper or you can't, and if you can't then you'll face the consequences.

GREG *gets up and walks across to* GLEN *whose head is down and who has tears in his eyes.*

GREG: I've got m'self into all kinds of shit today, mate, and this is going to get me into some more, but I have to tell you something. Your mother is one of the last persons in the world I'd deliberately hurt. When I sacked her I suffered. When I sacked you I suffered because

it was going to hurt her. Claire's not going to like what I just said but I've said it.
CLAIRE: Nothing I didn't know already.
GREG: If you believe what you heard today I'm nothing but a vain and stupid prick. But not so stupid that I didn't know what was going on. Julie told me about the whole set-up from go to whoa and I laughed along with everyone else. And in a way that makes me worse than any of them because I *knew* how sensitive you were about not having a girlfriend. Your mother broke down and cried one night about it. I don't think what you did was right. But I don't think what I did was right either.

The two men look at each other. GLEN *suddenly and involuntarily hugs* GREG. *There are tears in both men's eyes.*

GLEN: You woulda been a bloody better dad than the one I had.

There's a visible release of tension around the room. In the silence, JACK *scans the faces around the horseshoe and then scans them the other way. It's a moment of collective vulnerability and emotion and* JACK *holds up his hands so nobody will break the silence.*

JACK: Now what do we do about all this?
GLEN: Mr Baldoni, if you give me me job back I won't ever, ever do this sort of shit again. And I'll pay for the car.
JACK: Glen, we've talked about the problem of your short fuse and the feeling was it's not suddenly going to disappear. Greg's got to go away and think.
JULIE: Mac and Nookie were the troublemakers.
GREG: I've wanted to get rid of Mac and Nookie for years, but Richard tells me that everyone will walk if I try it.
LUKA: Bullshit. They'd bloody cheer.
CLAIRE: You've been complaining about them for years, Greg. If you haven't got the guts to finally do something then please don't ever complain about them again.
LUKA: Mr Baldoni. You put the rates up two dollars an hour and sack Nookie and Mac and nobody's gonna walk. Nobody.
GREG: Well, I'm not going to make any decisions here and now. It's not the time and it's not the place.
JACK: If that's what you feel.

GREG: Do *you* think it's the time and place?
JACK: It strikes me there's been quite a few things resolved today and it could be a good time to capitalise on that. We usually try and come up with an agreement.
GREG: I've got to go away and think about Glen.
JACK: What about Luka's point? A bit more communication between management and the workforce? Workplace meetings so everyone can exchange ideas and hear how the firm is travelling?
JULIE: And a weekly newsletter. My last firm did that. It was great.
THERESE: Give a summary of the monthly accounts.
RICHARD: Profit share bonuses for increased productivity.
GREG: Hang on!
JULIE: But none of this'll work until you get rid of Mac and Nookie. They'll just sneer at everything.
GREG: I'm not paying them huge redundancy packages!
JACK: Schedule them for one of my communication skills courses. They'll resign within half an hour. I promise.

Laughter.

GREG: Summary of the monthly accounts? So what I get paid is there for all to see.
THERESE: Switch a lot of your package to profit share like everyone else.
GREG: Listen, we haven't even said there'll be profit share yet. I'm not going to let myself be railroaded.
JACK: What do you want to see happen as a result of all this, Greg? It's got to seem fair to you. It's got to seem fair to everyone.
CLAIRE: Mac and Nookie go. Adrian goes back to university. Richard gets the manager's job he should've got.

Cheers and whistles from JULIE *and* THERESE.

JACK: Agreed Greg? Can I write that down?
CLAIRE: Yes, you can.
JACK: Greg?
GREG: Power behind the bloody throne.
CLAIRE: Well, you've been a little dethroned today, 'mate', haven't you?! Wages go up two dollars an hour.
JULIE: Newsletter.

THERESE: Profit share. Account disclosure.
RICHARD: Luka for foreman.
JACK: Is he the best?
LUKA: Bloody oath.
JACK: Greg, what do you think?
CLAIRE: Absolutely. He's delighted. Write it down.
JACK: Don't railroad him. He's got to sign this like everyone else.
GREG: [*gloomily*] Is there any way I wouldn't?
CLAIRE: And he sells that stupid yacht.
GREG: Hey! That's not part of this!
JACK: In all fairness, Claire, it isn't. That's an agreement you two are going to have to make. Now the tough one. Glen.
GLEN: [*really desperate*] Please give me me job back, Mr Baldoni. I promise I won't stuff up. I promise. I promise.
GREG: I can't decide right now, Glen.
JACK: If Greg did make you foreman, Luka, what would you say? About Glen?
LUKA: [*to* GLEN] Mate, I don't want to hurt you. But you are a bloody risk.
GLEN: No mate! We shook hands.
LUKA: Yeah, we shook hands. But, mate, it's a bit like workin' with a time bomb. And you never know what's gonna set you off.
GLEN: No mate. Not anymore.
LUKA: You're always going to be a bit like that, Glen. [*Pause. To* GREG] I think I could handle him, but the best thing would be a probation period.
JACK: You know what that means, Glen?
GLEN: I fuck up and I'm out.
JACK: Yep. Fuck up and you're out. No matter how much you like the job, fuck up and no one's going to listen. You're out.
GLEN: [*nodding vigorously*] Fuck up and I'm out.
CLAIRE: Six months probation.

> MAUREEN *hugs* CLAIRE.

GREG: Just go ahead. Pretend I'm not here. A year. One fuck-up in the year and you're out, Glen, okay?

> GLEN *nods vigorously and bobs up and down excitedly.*

GLEN: Let's have a drink. Hey? Let's get stuck into it!
JACK: I think you just about can, Glen. There's some drinks and food set up next door so we can have a bit of a talk about all this.

GLEN leaps up excitedly and hugs his mother.

GLEN: I got me job, I got me job, I got me job!
JACK: After we have something to eat and drink, if everyone's still happy we'll sign the agreement.

Everyone gets up and starts talking with animation as they head towards the next room. BARRY *moves towards* JACK.

BARRY: Well done, mate.
JACK: Keep your eye on him.
BARRY: We will.
JACK: Barry. Thanks for coming.

BARRY *gives* JACK *a friendly bash on the shoulder that nearly flattens him and leaves.* MAUREEN *comes across.*

MAUREEN: Thank you. I think that this's been one of the very best days of my life. I'm just glad you're not still working down the mines.
JACK: Actually I was a training officer on the surface, but I knew how tough it was below, and it gives me a bit of cred.
MAUREEN: You don't need any cred with me.
JACK: Your problems aren't over, Maureen. You've got a difficult boy.
MAUREEN: I know. But I haven't got a boy that's being turned into an animal in prison. Thanks.
JACK: It's not so much me. It's the process. It usually works.
MAUREEN: Sometimes it doesn't?
JACK: Sometimes I've had to break up fights. Sometimes I've got into 'em. But mostly it works. Better than the alternative. Go and have something to eat and drink. I'll just finish writing these notes and join you all.

MAUREEN *goes.* JULIE *approaches.*

JULIE: Are you sure you're married?
JACK: I wish I could say no.
JULIE: Are you sure your brother's a pig?
JACK: Absolute.
JULIE: Thanks for today.

JACK: It's a pleasure. It really has been. After a good one like this you go away thinking there's a huge reservoir of decency in the human species. We just somehow manage to stuff up most of the time.

JULIE: Why is that?

JACK: I'm still trying to work it out. My brother's not an *absolute* pig.

JULIE: What's he do?

JACK: He's a radiologist.

JULIE: [*raising her eyebrows*] I'll give you my number.

> JULIE *smiles and moves towards the other room as* JACK *keeps scribbling.* GLEN *runs back into the room.*

GLEN: Mum's giving me stick 'cause I forgot to thank you.

JACK: She's a great mum, Glen.

GLEN: She's the bloody best mate.

JACK: Next time you feel you're about to lose it, think about what it's going to do to her.

GLEN: Mate, that's great advice.

> *He shakes* JACK's *hand vigorously and runs back towards the next room. He stops and turns at the door.*

Mate, that's great advice.

> JACK *smiles and shakes his head as* GLEN *disappears. He listens to the sound of animated and friendly conversation coming from next door, looks down at the agreement he's scribbled and moves towards them all. He too disappears out the door leaving the stage empty. The sounds of conversation and bursts of laughter continue as the lights go down.*

THE END

A Conversation

Diane Craig (left) as Barbara and Deborah Kennedy as Coral in the 2001 Ensemble Theatre production in Sydney. (Photo: Robert McFarlane)

Thank you to Mark Rosenblatt, who directed a reading in the UK; Oz Scott, director of a US reading; and Sandra Bates, director of the original Australian production for their valuable contribution to the final version of the play.

DW

A Conversation was first produced by the Ensemble Theatre at the Ensemble Theatre, Sydney, on 5 September 2001, with the following cast:

JACK MANNING	Geoff Cartwright
DEREK MILSOM	Robert Coleby
BARBARA MILSOM	Diane Craig
LORIN ZEMANEK	Sandy Gore
MICK WILLIAMS	Glenn Hazeldine
CORAL WILLIAMS	Deborah Kennedy
BOB SHORTER	Greg McNeill
GAIL WILLIAMS	Bianca Rowe
VOICE OF SCOTT WILLIAMS	Damien Garvey

Director, Sandra Bates
Assistant Director, Andrew Doyle
Production Manager, Melissa Gray
Technical Manager, Matt Binnie

CHARACTERS

JACK MANNING, community conference convenor
DEREK MILSOM, late 40s
BARBARA MILSOM, mid-40s
LORIN ZEMANEK, early 40s
MICK WILLIAMS, early 20s
CORAL WILLIAMS, late 40s
BOB SHORTER, mid-50s
GAIL WILLIAMS, mid-20s
VOICE OF SCOTT WILLIAMS, mid-20s

Extract (on p.76) from 'The Sociobiology of Sociopathy: An Integrated Evolutionary Model' by Linda Mealey in *Behavioral and Brain Sciences*, Vol.18, No.3, New York: Cambridge University Press, 1995, reprinted with the permission of Cambridge University Press.

A hotel conference room. A little on the seedy side. Mid morning. JACK, *late thirties, arranges a horseshoe of chairs facing outwards towards the audience.* LORIN ZEMANEK, *clearly nervous, enters.* JACK *looks up.*

JACK: Lorin, thanks for coming.
LORIN: I nearly didn't.
    There's an awkward pause.
  Can you…?
JACK: What?
LORIN: Can you really be—?
JACK: Be?
LORIN: Do you *really* have as much faith in this community conferencing thing as you make out. I mean the way you sold it to me, it…
JACK: It what?
LORIN: Wonder cure.
JACK: I didn't say that.
LORIN: I've been thinking this through…
JACK: And?
LORIN: I have to say I have *real* doubts.
JACK: All I can hope is that what happens here might dispel some of them. Coffee?
LORIN: Thanks. [*As* JACK *pours her coffee*] Not to be rude, but have you ever facilitated a conference where the tensions are as extreme as these are going to be?
JACK: No.
LORIN: I have people in therapy for years before there's change, and in two hours you honestly expect—
JACK: This isn't therapy.
LORIN: —to get positive outcomes?
JACK: This isn't therapy.
LORIN: So you said. But I'm still not sure what it *is*.
JACK: It tries to reduce conflict between people. It doesn't heal psyches.
LORIN: Tries.
JACK: Yes, tries. Tries to allow people to stop hating or obsessing or being angry and enraged and get on with their lives.
LORIN: It's going to help the Milsoms get on with their lives?

JACK: I hope so.
LORIN: I remain to be convinced.

> *She looks sceptical and exhales.* JACK *makes some marginal adjustments to the seating.*

I'm going to be the scapegoat.
JACK: We talked about this.
LORIN: It's one thing to talk about it in abstract. It's another thing when it's just about to happen.
JACK: I know that. I really appreciate the fact you're here.
LORIN: I did my job to the best of my ability.
JACK: I know.
LORIN: If I'm attacked unfairly I'll defend myself. I don't accept that I'm totally to blame.
JACK: I don't think anyone will think that.
LORIN: Yes they will.

> DEREK *and* BARBARA MILSOM *enter.* DEREK *is in his late forties,* BARBARA *a little younger.* DEREK *is agitated and strides ahead of his wife. He sees* LORIN, *but ignores her and only nods briefly at* JACK *as he unwraps a large beautifully-framed photograph of a young woman of about twenty. He holds the photo behind his back, face towards the audience, as he ponders where to put it.*

JACK: Glad you could come, Derek.
DEREK: Where will they be sitting?

> JACK *indicates.*

JACK: Glad you came, Barbara.
BARBARA: I'm not sure what good it'll do to rake over all this again.
DEREK: I want them to see the person their son killed. It's okay if I put daughter's photo here?
JACK: You do what you feel you want to do.
DEREK: I want them to see her. I want them to see her every second they're in this room.
BARBARA: It's provocative, Derek.
DEREK: It's meant to be.

> DEREK *props the photo up on the ground in front of the left-hand chairs, using the backing prop attached.* BARBARA *feels that politeness dictates they can't ignore* LORIN *any longer.*

BARBARA: Hi Lorin.
LORIN: Hi Barbara, Derek.

DEREK glares at LORIN *with patent hostility, then turns to* JACK.

DEREK: So where are they? They called this conference, so where are they?
JACK: They've got further to come.

DEREK unloads a pile of books and folders from a briefcase he is carrying. JACK *looks at him.* DEREK *looks at* JACK.

DEREK: Maybe they stopped off to rob a few houses on the way. [*Indicating the pile*] I'm going to talk straight on all of this. If anyone tries to dispute what I say I want to have all the facts on hand.
BARBARA: Derek, all the facts in the world aren't going to bring her back.
DEREK: I want that family to understand what we've lost.
JACK: [*looking at his watch*] Is the traffic bad out there?
LORIN: [*simultaneously*] Yes, terrible.
DEREK: [*simultaneously*] Traffic's fine.

There's an awkward silence as they work out how to deal with this total contradiction.

LORIN: I had to come over the bridge.
DEREK: So did we.
LORIN: Seemed heavy to me, but I don't usually do this at this time of day.
DEREK: Traffic was fine.
BARBARA: Bumper to bumper, Derek.
DEREK: But flowing. *They're* not coming over the bridge in any case. They come from out west.
JACK: [*nodding*] They've got a long way to come.
DEREK: Then they leave earlier. It's called organising your time.

There's a silence. Then CORAL WILLIAMS, *a woman in her late forties, pokes her head into the room. She's not dressed well or fashionably.*

CORAL: Hey, is this it? Yeah, this is it.

She turns and beckons and MICK WILLIAMS, 22, GAIL WILLIAMS, 26, *and* BOB SHORTER, 55, *enter. There's an awkward bout of head nodding and a few desultory 'hi's. The* WILLIAMS *family are ill at ease under the hostile glare of* DEREK *and* BARBARA.

BOB: [*to* CORAL] Call me on your mobile when you're finished here and I'll come and get you.

JACK: You're Bob?

BOB: Yeah.

JACK: Recognised your voice. You're not staying?

BOB: I thought it over and—no.

JACK: It would help.

BOB: [*looking at the* MILSOMS] Scott did something I can't condone in any shape or form. I don't want to be sitting around here trying to find excuses.

JACK: I don't think anyone will be trying to find excuses.

CORAL: I didn't come to make excuses.

BOB: Frankly I can't see the sense in this and I've got a business to run.

JACK: If you stay it'll help. Believe me.

CORAL: [*to* BOB] You were his uncle for God's sake, Bob.

BOB *looks at his watch, looks at* CORAL, *and sighs.*

BOB: Okay, but I'm not making excuses.

CORAL: Neither am I. He did what he did and if there's anyone to blame it's me.

GAIL: Mum, don't keep saying that.

JACK: Okay, let's start. The Williams family—Coral, Gail, would you mind sitting here? Mick, Bob, just there. Barbara, Derek, on the other side of me, and Lorin just here next to where I'll be. Ground rules. You can get up and move around any time you feel you want to. No violence and secondly this isn't going to work if anyone walks out before it's over.

Everyone goes to their allotted seats in silence. JACK *sits himself in the middle. He waits thirty seconds while the shuffling segues into total frozen silence. The* WILLIAMS *family stares at the portrait of Donna.*

You all know why we're here. Coral was told about community conferences by one of her friends and phoned me and asked me to organise one for the two families involved. I've spoken to all of you and although some were reluctant at first—

GAIL: You're not kidding.
CORAL: Gail!
JACK: —you've all agreed to come tonight.
GAIL: [*looking at the* MILSOMS] They're just going to unload on us again. We've been through it once at the trial!
CORAL: Gail, will you just shut your mouth for once in your life.
GAIL: Well, what bloody good will it do?
CORAL: Gail!
JACK: Gail, I'm hoping it *will* do some good. Your lives have all crossed in a way that's caused great pain. What we're attempting tonight is a conversation to hear what happened, to hear how people have been affected, and to see if we can make some sense out of it all.

He waits another ten seconds or so. Again there's absolute stillness, absolute tension.

Normally the perpetrator of the crime begins by telling us what happened in their own words. I initially suggested that this conference be conducted in prison but Barbara and Derek didn't want Scott to be there in person.
CORAL: Neither did I.
JACK: But they did agree to let me record Scott telling us his version of events. Scott, as you know, is in the prison hospital at the moment, but he did do the recording on the understanding that what we hear tonight is strictly confidential. Is that agreed?
BARBARA: I've thought about this, Jack. I don't think I want to hear.
DEREK: Neither do I.
JACK: For this to work it's much better if we do.
DEREK: Why?
JACK: We need to know how Scott feels about what he did, because that usually alters the way we feel about him.
DEREK: He's made some attempt to *justify* what he did?
JACK: [*nodding*] In his own way.
DEREK: I can't believe that.
BARBARA: Justify?
JACK: In his own way.

There's another tense pause.

DEREK: Okay, let's hear it.

JACK: He's been totally frank. What you're about to hear isn't going to be pretty.

> DEREK *looks at* BARBARA *who finally nods.* JACK *turns on the tape.*

SCOTT: [*voice only*] 'I saw Donna when she came into the supermarket where I had a job lugging boxes and stacking shelves. She didn't ever see me, but I kept seeing her. I done all those things they taught me in prison. I looked away, went out the back, pulled out the cards. I read how I hated prison, how I never wanted to go back, but I was getting hot. Every night I'm jerking off three or four times. I hold out for a week but it's getting real bad and I take out the cards 'cause I know they've got Lorin's number on and I'm just about to call her, but I know it's no use. I go to Donna's place and follow a guy through the security door with flowers in my hand like I'm delivering them and wait for her behind a corner. As soon as she had the key in the lock I had the knife at her throat. She didn't make a sound. I taped her mouth and her hands and took off her jeans and undies. I showed her the pictures in the magazines. Chicks with bruises. Tied up and loving it. They said in court I hit her because I was in a rage. It's bullshit. I wasn't in a rage. I wanted her to get off on it. Lorin told us that chick's don't really like rough stuff, but by now I'm believing what I want to believe, and I start thinkin' that Lorin is wrong in any case 'cause Donna is comin' every time I put it in.'

DEREK: I'm out of here.

> JACK *switches off the tape.* DEREK *gets up to walk out, beckoning* BARBARA. JACK *moves in front of him.*

JACK: Please.

DEREK: You expect me to listen to that?

LORIN: It happens in lots of rapes, Derek. Sexual arousal is not much different to terror, physiologically.

DEREK: It's filth. It's lies.

LORIN: The body is built to respond to certain stimuli. If the levels of arousal are high enough— [there's nothing she could have done about it.]

BARBARA: What are you telling us, Lorin? She enjoyed being beaten to death?

LORIN: Barbara, it was just a reflex— [She was terrified.]
BARBARA: I can't listen to that.
LORIN: She was terrified, Barbara. Make no mistake. She was terrified.
DEREK: You want to know how terrified? I'll tell you. I've done research. Lots of it. You want to know what she went through?
JACK: We'll get to that, Derek. Painful as it is, let's just finish this.
DEREK: You want to know what she really went through?
JACK: [*holding up his hand, palm outward*] Derek.

DEREK *sits.* JACK *switches on the tape again.*

SCOTT: [*voice only*] 'I'm crazy by now and I can't stop myself giving her more.'
DEREK: Your kid's a monster. I'm sorry, your kid's a monster.

JACK *switches off the tape.*

MICK: You think we don't know that? Why the fuck do you think we're here tonight?
GAIL: You're not here to sell out your brother.
MICK: I'm not here to pretend he was a saint, either.

From left: Robert Coleby as Derek, Sandy Gore as Lorin, Diane Craig as Barbara and Geoff Cartwright as Jack in the 2001 Ensemble Theatre production in Sydney. (Photo: Robert McFarlane)

JACK: Can we try and finish this?

There's a silence. JACK *switches on the tape.*

SCOTT: [*voice only*] 'But I didn't ever mean to kill her. Honest. No way. I didn' realise I was hitting her that hard, you got to believe that. And I swear she was alive when I left. I didn' know about the bleeding inside. I got just as much a shock as anyone when I heard it on the news. I didn't mean for her to die. I thought about her every day and night for weeks. She was beautiful. She was my dream girl. I didn't ever want her dead. You got to believe that. I didn't mean to take your daughter away. So, sorry.'

There's a silence as they all digest this.

DEREK: [*to* JACK] That's supposed to make us feel better?

BARBARA: That sick, sick story is supposed to make us feel better?

JACK: Coral, who's been affected by your son's action?

CORAL: Everyone in this room and many more.

JACK: Who's been most affected?

CORAL: Mr and Mrs Milsom. That's the reason I wanted to meet them face to face. I just wanted to say I'm sorry. I've been wanting to say it ever since the courtroom. I saw them crying day after day. And I cried too. For their girl. I don't know what I did wrong bringin' up that boy, but it's pretty plain I made a bloody mess of it. What he did was shocking beyond words, and a lot of it has to be my fault, so that's what I'm here for. To say I'm sorry I wasn't a better mother and I'm sorry for all your pain.

GAIL: We're all sorry. Really sorry. We hate what Scott did.

CORAL: I thought if we came here tonight then…

JACK: Then what?

CORAL: Mr and Mrs Milsom, I know you probably want my boy to suffer as much as humanly possible, but I thought that maybe…

DEREK: Maybe what?

CORAL: He bloody near died after this attack and when he's sent back to prison they'll do it again. I don't want him out of prison. Ever. But they're going to kill him and the prison authorities are doing nothing.

GAIL: 'Course they're doing nothing. They want him dead.

CORAL: They're saying it was only a one-off thing but we know it's not. The only way he's going t'stay alive is if they put him in protective custody.

GAIL: Protective custody costs a fortune. It's cheaper if he's dead.
DEREK: What's this leading to, Coral?
CORAL: I thought if you saw how truly sorry we are about your girl, you might say you've no objection to him being put in protective custody. Our lawyer said it'd help his case. He says that if a serious offender's conditions are going to be changed the victim's family has to be consulted.
JACK: Coral, this is really not appropriate.
DEREK: [*to* CORAL] You can't be serious.
BARBARA: We'd help your son?
CORAL: I thought if you saw how sorry we were—
DEREK: [*to* CORAL] You honestly think that Barbara and I—
JACK: Coral, this isn't the agenda we're here for today.
CORAL: I want him to pay for what he did, but I don't want him to die. No mother wants their son to die.
JACK: Coral, if you were going to bring this up you should have told me.
CORAL: He was only stabbed last week!
JACK: You should have rung me and told me.
GAIL: Mum, are you crazy? They're never going to help us.
CORAL: [*to* BARBARA] I know it's an awful lot to ask, but no mother ever born can sit round and do nothing if her son's going t'die.
DEREK: So this meeting's nothing to do with being sorry?
CORAL: It is, it is. I set this thing up before Scott was stabbed. I set this up to tell you how sorry I was. It's been preying on my mind and drivin' me crazy.
GAIL: Mum, get real.
DEREK: Coral, do you want to know how I really feel?
JACK: Let's not pursue this now.
DEREK: I think the prisoners who stabbed your son deserve a medal. My only regret is that they only half did the job.
GAIL: Mum, let's just get out've here.
CORAL: You've lost a daughter. You know how it feels.
DEREK: Your son *killed* our daughter.
JACK: Coral, let's not pursue this.
DEREK: Now or ever again. [*To* CORAL] Have you any idea what a nightmare this has been for us. From the moment we first heard?

JACK: How *did* you feel when you first heard, Derek?
DEREK: It's the scene from hell that no parent ever wants to happen. The police. The look. A scream inside you because you know what the cop is there for.
BARBARA: I did scream. I just lost it. For days. I just lost it.
DEREK: You think, 'No! Please tell me it's wrong. Please tell me she's hurt. She's in the hospital, fine. But not that.' No parent should ever have to hear that. No one should ever, ever have to hear that.
BARBARA: I couldn't walk. I couldn't do anything but cry.
DEREK: I had to support her at the funeral.
BARBARA: I was fine at the funeral. I cried. It's not a crime.
JACK: How've you been since, Barbara?
BARBARA: I still cry every day. Nightmares every night. Derek does too, but he can tell you about that.
JACK: Nightmares every night?

> BARBARA *nods.*

Could you tell us about them?
BARBARA: I'm at the hospital like I was that night. Holding my dead girl's hand. Looking at her battered body and crying. And suddenly her eyes open and she's alive. And I'm weeping with joy. Cradling her head in my arms. And I wake up yelling that she's alive...
JACK: How's it affected your life? In other ways?
DEREK: In other ways? In every way.
BARBARA: I had to resign my job. I'm a teacher. I *was* a teacher. I loved my job. I never had a problem. But suddenly I found myself sitting in front of my class with tears pouring down my face. And that was it. I knew I couldn't teach anymore. I knew I was finished. They shifted me out of the classroom into admin but I couldn't concentrate for longer than a minute or two. I took anti-depressants but they just made me feel numb—which I already was in any case. I can't relate to people anymore. They're not part of my world. I hate them because they haven't had it happen to them. I'm not part of *any* world anymore.
CORAL: I'm sorry. I really am.
LORIN: [*to* BARBARA] You've been through an extreme trauma. These things don't just fade away.

DEREK: Ten years down the track we're going to be just as screwed up as we are tonight.
LORIN: You need intensive grief counselling. With all due respect, a quick-fix solution like tonight won't help much.
BARBARA: I've had grief counselling up to my ears, Lorin. [*To* CORAL] Do you know how much I loved Donna? Do you know how much she was part of my life? I see daughter from hell movies everywhere, but this was no daughter from hell—
DEREK: This was a kid who was friendly and loving—
BARBARA: When she was in primary school the teacher said, 'Yeah she's bright, but look at this'. And she showed us a sociogram. A graph with arrows showing which kids wanted to be friends with which. And all the arrows—
DEREK: Pointed to Donna.
BARBARA: [*illustrating with her hands*] These arrows going—whoosh—straight at Donna. And the teacher says, 'One thing you can be sure of—'
DEREK: '—your girl is going to have a very happy life.'
BARBARA: How many mothers have a daughter who's also your best friend? Who tells you everything? And you tell her everything? I had one. I had one. I used to love watching her laugh. It made me feel better than anything in the world. When my girl was happy, I was over the moon. Yes, I had a career and all that, but the moments that lit up my life were those moments when I saw my daughter laugh.
DEREK: You want us to help save your son when we've just heard him telling us that killing Donna was an accident? He only meant to leave her a wreck?
BARBARA: She lit up my life.
DEREK: His dream girl? Dream girl? Well, that's one hell of a sick dream, and that's one hell of a sick son. And at the end he tags on two words. 'So, sorry.' Hey? 'So, sorry.' Are we supposed to take that seriously? Are we supposed to say, 'Well that's great, let's all shake hands'? 'I'll sign that petition'?
GAIL: If he gets protective custody he's still going to spend the rest of his life in jail. Isn't that enough?
DEREK: Frankly, no.

GAIL: What *would* make you happy? Hung by the neck by piano wire?
DEREK: If I was given the chance I'd be happy to kill him myself. I'd like to put a gun to his head and shoot him.
CORAL: There's one dead already. Does it really help to make it two?
BARBARA: He shows her a pornographic S and M magazine when she's tied up and helpless and thinks it'll get her excited? Can anyone be *that* far removed from reality?
DEREK: Does he really deserve to live?
CORAL: I don't want him to die.
BARBARA: Have you any understanding of just how much *this* mother misses her daughter, Coral? Have you *any* understanding?

She breaks down and tears roll down her face.

JACK: You have nightmares too, Derek?
DEREK: [*nodding*] She's dead. She's haemorrhaging blood. But he's there. Staring at me. And I'm throwing punches. But they're not quite landing. Never quite landing. And I wake up crying out in rage.
JACK: In what other ways has your life been affected?
DEREK: My life is over. I'm in a moon suit, jumping over barren silver rocks in slow motion. No one else out there.
LORIN: You've got each other.
DEREK: We're filing for divorce. There's nothing left. I used to love my work. Now I'm just going through the motions.

There's a silence.

GAIL: Have you ever considered that your work was part of the problem?
CORAL: Gail!
GAIL: Exactly how much do you pay the women you employ?
CORAL: Gail, please.
GAIL: Mum, I didn't come here to crawl on my belly. A terrible thing happened but Scott wasn't born a monster. No one is born that way. If he turned out that way then there've got to be reasons.
DEREK: What in the hell has what I pay my workers got to do with my daughter's death?
GAIL: Mum no sooner gets in the door here tonight and she's blaming herself. But how in the hell could she be any kind of mother to Scott when she's working for next to nothing for a non-union industrial cleaning firm sixty-five hours a week to keep us all alive.

DEREK: If that's the sort of logic you're going to use we might as well stop the whole exercise.

GAIL: Scott wasn't born bad. There were factors.

DEREK: And one of them is *not* what I pay my female workers.

BOB: Gail, I probably pay my girls the same as Derek. It's the going rate. Are you going to start blaming me?

GAIL: This whole society created Scott and yes, you're part of it too, Uncle Bob.

CORAL: Gail, don't talk to your uncle like that. Whenever we had our backs to the wall, who helped us? He did.

BOB: It was my money got you through bloody university, young lady.

GAIL: And I'm grateful, but it nearly made me sick when I heard you boasting at Granny's funeral how you'd screwed your workers 'good and proper' in your latest workplace agreement.

BOB: Everyone tries to do the best for themselves.

GAIL: And how you wouldn't have anyone who belonged to a union near the place.

BOB: I give you a lift here, 'cause Mick's pranged his car, I agree to stay, and this is what happens. Typical of you, young lady. If I paid my girls more than anyone else I'd've gone bankrupt and where would you be then?

DEREK: If this is going to turn into an exercise of blaming everyone else but Scott then we're out of here.

CORAL: If there's anyone to blame it's me.

GAIL: Mum, there are many, many factors.

BOB: Yeah, well I'm certainly not one of them. Your mother and I had nothing as kids. No education. Nothing. And building a business from that is bloody hard.

CORAL: You've always done the right thing by us, Bob.

BOB: No one could've done anything for Scott. He was wild from the time he could crawl. You had to tell him twenty times not to do somethin' an' it made no damn difference. You'd tell him off and he'd fly into a rage.

GAIL: He had an impulse control problem. So do thousands of other kids and they don't murder people.

BOB: Exactly. How come Mick didn't fly off the handle when you told him 'No!'?

DEREK: Exactly.

CORAL: I didn't come here tonight to look for excuses. My boy did a terrible thing, but I still love him.

DEREK: Maybe you should listen to what this boy you 'love' left out of his little story.

BARBARA: Derek, do we have to?

DEREK: I want them to hear. I want to remind them what their boy actually did! And then ask whether any 'factors' can ever excuse it. [*He fishes in his pile of documents, holds up the coroner's report, then reads.*] Her spleen was ruptured, her kidneys were bruised, five ribs were cracked, her lung was punctured and she was bleeding internally from at least five different locations. Her rectum was ripped by a Coke bottle, another little detail your boy omitted to tell us. Her skull was also fractured and this is the wound that caused the brain haemorrhage that probably killed her.

> *He puts down the report and looks at the* WILLIAMS *family. He picks up another report.*

The thing we go through life trusting is that if we don't provoke someone, they won't harm us. That if we're defenceless and we look someone in the eyes they'll be decent enough not to harm us. We couldn't live if we didn't have that much trust. Now here's someone looking my daughter in the eyes and making it quite clear that despite the fact she's done absolutely nothing to him, he's going to kill her. This provokes fear of the most intense kind it is possible for a human being to have. It's way outside our range of human expectation. [*He flicks through the report and reads.*] The heart rate spikes up temporarily to three hundred beats a minute and all senses except vision shut down, and vision becomes tunnel vision.

> *He stops reading and looks at the* WILLIAMS *family.*

Donna would have been faintly aware of the sounds of her own body being broken to bits, but all she would have seen were the eyes of her killer. And all she could do, with her hands bound and her mouth gagged, was hope that the terror in her eyes would strike some chord of compassion. Which of course it didn't. Thankfully while it was happening she wouldn't've felt pain. At these levels of arousal everything except terror is blotted out, but when your son had had his fun and left her, the pain would have come flooding through her to a degree we can't even start to imagine. One cracked rib is enough to keep most of us up at night, but her injuries, coming after the terror she'd been through, would have been so intense that her body probably died hours before it had to to spare her the unendurable. That's the reality. That's the reality of how my daughter died. That's the reality to stand alongside the sick fantasy that your son convinced himself was happening. Can any of you sit here and listen to that reality and give us a reason why we shouldn't feel *elated* if your son dies? Can you?

GAIL: Okay, it's horrible. Horrible. But there *were* factors.

DEREK: To hell with your factors. Look at her photo there and just sit and think about how she died.

GAIL: [*quietly, after a pause*] There were factors.

There's a silence. Tears are still flowing from BARBARA*'s eyes, but* DEREK*'s eyes are dry and cold with fury.*

JACK: Coral, it must have been hard for you to listen to that?

CORAL: My boy did a terrible, terrible thing. Be easier if I could hate him, but I can't. I know he's bad. He was always bad. Always lying an' stealing, getting into fights. And if he hurt you he'd say he was sorry, but you knew damn well he wasn't. But there was something you had to like about him. He was funny and full of life.

MICK: [*sardonically*] Yeah.

CORAL: Mick, I said he did a terrible, terrible thing. I know that. I know.

There's a pause.

JACK: Lorin, is there anything you'd like to say?

LORIN: I know a lot of you here are blaming me—

DEREK: You were the one who sent him back out onto the streets.

LORIN: That's not actually—

GAIL: Before he was ready.

LORIN: I didn't send him back out on the streets. The parole panel made a decision. They heard what I had to say and what two other court-appointed psychiatrists had to say and they made their decision. I wasn't the only voice they listened to.

DEREK: The two other psychiatrists said it was too risky to release him but you told the panel he was ready.

LORIN: I said what I truly thought and I stressed the risks. The parole board had all the information. *They* made the decision.

DEREK: You'd been treating Scott for five hundred hours. The other two 'experts' had only seen him for two hours each. Of course they were going to give your report more weight.
LORIN: I stressed the risks.
DEREK: [*contemptuously*] Yeah.
LORIN: I said on balance he should be released but only under *strict* parole supervision.
CORAL: Strict supervision. What a joke!
MICK: He goes off to the parole officer once a week, tells a few lies and that's it. Strict supervision?
LORIN: I insisted on three visits a week.
MICK: So how come he only came once?
LORIN: My recommendation was ignored as part of a cost-cutting exercise. But I didn't know this.
DEREK: Shouldn't you have?
LORIN: They didn't notify me.
DEREK: Why didn't you check?
LORIN: I meant to. I was overworked. But I should have. I should have.
CORAL: In a few days he's stealing my money and his brother's money and his uncle's money and buying more filthy magazines and locking himself in his room. And I don't need to tell you what he was doin' in there. The parole officer says, 'How's he doing?' and you can see from his eyes he doesn't give a damn. And I say, 'He's buying those magazines and videos again', and he says, 'Well, if he does anything worrying, get in touch'. And I say, 'It *is* worrying that he's buying those things again', an' he says, 'Don't worry. He's had therapy. He knows women don't like that sort of stuff. He'll be fine.'
LORIN: I should have been told immediately. I was reasonably confident he'd been cured of his obsession with violent sex, but I specifically asked to be told if there was any evidence that it was recurring.
DEREK: And what exactly would you have done?
LORIN: I would've realised he needed more intensive therapy.
DEREK: More of the treatment that had done absolutely *nothing* to change him?
LORIN: It had changed him.
DEREK: If you'd read your own literature you'd have realised that there is no hard evidence that high levels of violent sexual preoccupation are *ever* cured by the 'let's sit down and talk about this' approach.

LORIN: The studies are inconclusive.
DEREK: You'd want them to be wouldn't you, or you'd all be out of a job.
LORIN: I believed in the work I did and I did it to the best of my ability.
CORAL: Yeah, and look what happened.
DEREK: [*to* CORAL, *pointing at* LORIN] You could have rung Lorin yourself. *You* could have told her he was buying that porn again.
CORAL: He'd just got out of prison. I didn' want to do anything that might send him back there.
DEREK: You say Lorin let him out too early, but *you* wouldn't put him back? Where's the logic?
CORAL: I thought I could handle him.
MICK: [*to* CORAL] You'd yell at him once or twice and then let him do whatever the hell it was he wanted. Same as always.
CORAL: I've been workin' sixty hours a week from the time you were born to give you all a chance in life. How much energy am I supposed to have?
MICK: You didn't work hard on account of me. You were workin' long hours so Gail could get a B.A. or Masters or whatever the hell it is.
GAIL: What are saying, Mick? All this happened because I went to uni?
MICK: You didn' even take a part-time job. Not once. And then what'd you do? Run out on us as soon as you damn well could.
GAIL: I didn't take a part-time job because I was doing Honours. If you scrape through these days you don't even get a job. And what am I supposed to do? Stay in the house I was born in the rest of my life?
MICK: You were his older sister. You could've helped keep him in line. You blame everyone else, but you're part of the equation too.
GAIL: You stayed home, and what did you ever do to stop your brother?
MICK: Me? Whoever would've listened to me? All those years growin' up, Scott was the hero in our house.
CORAL: Scott was never a hero. That's stupid talk.
MICK: [*to* CORAL] He lies, he cheats, he gets himself half killed in fights. And what do you say? To me? What do you say? 'No one's ever gonna push Scott around.' Like hey, Mick, you poor dork. Stand up for yourself and beat the hell out've anyone that looks sideways at you like your brother Scott.
CORAL: I didn't meant it like that.

MICK: Whenever he'd do something bad, you'd laugh.
CORAL: He had a way of making things sound funny.
MICK: Oh yeah. Like, 'I hit him an' he went down and bounced up again, so I hit him again and he went down and bounced up *again*—' He puts a guy in hospital and let's all have a great big laugh.
CORAL: All boys have fights.
MICK: Oh yeah. He puts a guy in hospital so let's all have a great big laugh.
CORAL: I didn't know he was in hospital.
MICK: Even when he done his first rape at seventeen, you were full of excuses. 'Those girls. They lead young boys on.'
CORAL: It wasn't rape. He wasn't convicted.
MICK: You know something. You weren't *really* mad at him. Ever.
CORAL: I was as mad as hell. But I forgave. He had a way of talkin' you round. He talked Lorin around and she's supposed to be a bloody professional.

Sandy Gore as Lorin in the 2001 Ensemble Theatre production in Sydney. (Photo: Robert McFarlane)

DEREK: Some professional.

LORIN: Derek, you've made your point. Many times.

DEREK: They let him out because you said it was an 'acceptable' risk.

LORIN: He *was* making progress with me. The two psychiatrists just labelled him a paraphiliac and that was it.

DEREK: Lorin, would you tell us exactly what a paraphiliac is?

LORIN: It's a rapist who acts out violent sexual fantasies. And there's no doubt that that's how Scott first presented.

DEREK: And that's what Scott remained.

LORIN: Reverted to. There's a difference.

DEREK: Reverted, remained. What difference?

BARBARA: Our daughter's still dead.

DEREK: Those two clinicians thought he was still a paraphiliac. And they were right.

LORIN: I kept stressing the risks.

DEREK: You told the board how he played the role of someone trying to talk his buddy out of raping a woman, and had tears in his eyes.

LORIN: He did. He *finally* understood how devastating rape is to a woman. He understood. At that moment he understood.

BARBARA: And you told the board how he did exceptionally well in his *empathy* training. How he read the police reports of how upset his victims were. And how he cried. And how he sat down and wrote letters of apology to all his four victims. Never mailed of course, but he did it. He did it.

LORIN: They were sincere. His tears were real. I still can't understand why he didn't pick up the phone and call me that day.

DEREK: Because he's compulsively addicted to violent sex. And he's a sociopath. Which those two clinicians managed to pick up in the space of two hours as against your five hundred. And you sneered at their suggestion of direct behavioural deconditioning.

LORIN: That just treats the symptoms. It doesn't get to the root cause.

BARBARA: The root cause wasn't some terrible trauma in childhood. There was no evidence whatsoever that Scott had ever been molested or abused.

MICK: He hadn't. He was just born bad.

GAIL: Mick!

LORIN: The worst people are ever *born* with is a predisposition. No one is born bad.

DEREK: No one? Let's just qualify that a little. [*He reaches for a book and opens it at a page marked by a yellow marker strip.*] 'Behavioral and Brain Sciences'. Volume 18, Number 3. [*He reads.*] In every known culture 'sociopaths comprise three to four percent of the male population'. They're 'egocentric, aggressive, impulsive, and underneath a superficial veneer of sociability and charm, experience no love, shame, empathy, guilt or remorse'. And the evidence shows there's a strong genetic factor.

LORIN: Some genetic influence.

DEREK: Every twin study that's been done shows up to *half* of it *is*.

LORIN: The other half is what I use my professional skills to work on.

DEREK: There *are* people who are born bad. Or at least halfway bad. And he was one of them.

LORIN: A predisposition is just that, Derek, a predisposition. *Nothing* is fixed in concrete by the genes.

GAIL: [*to* DEREK] If you had had to live where we grew up you'd realise why there was such a high chance Scott would go off the rails.

DEREK: Don't give me that 'underprivileged' garbage. Your brother was a sociopath who became heavily addicted to violent sex. He was a walking time bomb and she [*pointing to* LORIN] let him back out on the streets.

BARBARA: What you can't admit, Lorin, is that you misdiagnosed, mistreated and misrepresented your patient.

DEREK: And you were paid five hundred times eighty dollars to do it!

LORIN: Scott had made considerable progress. Then he reverted. And I wasn't told.

BARBARA: [*quietly*] Lorin, are you ever going to accept *any* of the blame?

LORIN: I've accepted a lot of blame, believe me.

DEREK: Lorin, how many patients you treat have raped more than once? Before they were twenty-one? [*He picks up another folder.*] Just let me read you these statistics.

LORIN: I know the statistics, Derek.

DEREK: Let me refresh your memory then. If a rapist has offended against more than one victim then the chance of any therapy working is *eight* times less than if he'd offended against only one.

LORIN: I was aware of that, and knew it would make my work much harder.

DEREK: If violence is an integral part of the rape the chances are that on subsequent rapes the violence levels will escalate.
LORIN: Yes.
DEREK: No warning bells.
LORIN: Loud warning bells.
DEREK: In your own report— [*He holds up the report.*] Did you read his cynicism and anti-social scores on the MMPI? Did you read his levels on the attraction to sexual aggression scale?
LORIN: Of course.
DEREK: Very, *very* loud warning bells I would have thought.
LORIN: Yes. But I still refused to believe that Scott was beyond help. I still refuse to believe it. And I did help him. But he reverted and I should have been told. That's all I can say. And I'm more sorry than you can imagine about Donna, but I can't help you anymore here today.

She gets up to go. JACK *stands in her way.*

JACK: Lorin, they're saying things they feel they have to say. I know it's hard on you, but it'll help enormously if you stay.
LORIN: *Tell* me how it's going to help enormously, Jack?
JACK: This process needs everyone integral to all this hurt and anger to be here.
LORIN: Sorry, but I don't see one skerrick of evidence that anything has or will be achieved here today. Other than that people who are already devastated and angry are getting more devastated and angry. And people who are desperate and guilty are getting more desperate and guilty.
JACK: This process needs all that anger and hate and fear to be expressed. Give it a chance.
LORIN: And risk walking out even *more* demoralised than it's already made me? No thanks. [*She turns to go again.*] None of you will believe, or don't want to believe, how much I have suffered over this. Scott was making progress, but you're right. I was over-optimistic. I should have rung up the parole officer and checked. And your daughter is dead. For which I am hugely sorry. Believe me. Hugely sorry. But other times I get it right. I could have given you another folder. One that lists all my successes. Rapists who

have *never* re-offended. Child molesters who have never re-offended—I've got one of the highest success rates in this country. I got it wrong in *this case.*

She turns to go again.

JACK: Lorin, if you walk out the conference is over. Any chance of reducing the anguish all of you are going through is over.

LORIN: Reducing? You call this reducing?

JACK: [*toughly*] Lorin, you've got your particular skills, and you believe in them as you've made clear. I've got skills too and most of the time they work too. Now okay, this is a tough one. Tougher than I've ever had, but at least give me a chance and give the rest of us here a chance. Will you pay me at least *that* amount of professional respect?

MICK: Everyone's lookin' for someone to blame, Lorin, and you're just a convenient target. For God's sake, it was Scott who did this thing. Scott's to blame.

JACK: You didn't have to come here today, Lorin, but you did. Do you think it could be because you need to be here just as much as anyone else?

LORIN *looks at him.*

LORIN: Okay. Okay, Jack. I just hope you really do know what you're doing because right now I'm feeling pretty low.

She resumes her seat.

MICK: [*to* LORIN] Scott's to blame. Not you. If he wasn't such a bastard none of us would be here.

GAIL: Mick.

MICK: It's true. I got him a job, right? I talked the boss into it. So what does he do? He uses the job to look for his next victim. She'd come into the supermarket and I saw her too and I thought yeah, she's beautiful, and I remember just how beautiful when I look at that photo there. And then I see Scott looking and I take him and slam him against a wall and say *no!* And he grins like he always does and says, 'Hey, I don't do that stuff anymore'. And here's where I'm no better than you, Lorin. I half believed. He was such a good liar, I half believed. But when I hear it on the radio I know it's Scott. No doubt in the world. And I want to kill him. If it's bad being the brother of a rapist it's ten times worse being the brother of a killer. A sick killer. Wherever I go I can hear them thinking. Same family. Same blood. Don't let him near my daughter.

GAIL: Mick, that's rubbish.

MICK: It's fine for you, but I'm a bloke. Do you think there's anyone who knows me or has even heard about me, that thinks of me as Mick? Well I'll tell you something, they don't. I'm Scott's brother. That's who I am and I hate that.

GAIL: It's nothing to do with 'bad blood'.

MICK: Oh yeah, Gail. You've been to university. You're taught it's never anyone's fault—there are always 'factors'. But with Scott the biggest 'factor' is that he was born without a heart.

CORAL: Mick!

MICK: I'm five years old. Big bow and arrow. Metal tip right at my chest. Ice cold eyes. Did it every day, Mum, 'til I begged for mercy and pissed my pants. Every day for nearly a year. Scott's got a heart? Yeah, sure.

CORAL: All kids bully their little brothers!

MICK: You're still doing it, Mum. Still covering for him. Mr and Mrs Milsom, I don't know why the rest of my family are here, but I really did come to say I'm sorry. I just want to tell you that I hate my brother as much as you do. I hate him for what he is and what he's done. Ever since he was little, if he saw something he wanted he took it. To hell with the pain it caused anyone else. If Scott wanted he took. Lorin, you're not to blame. The little shit fooled you like he fooled so many people. He laughed about those 'empathy' sessions. He laughed about how he made tears come out of his eyes when he was writing his 'apologies'.

LORIN: He was sincere. *At the time.*

MICK: Yeah, well he forgot it real quick because with me it was the same old shit. 'Mick, they love the rough stuff. Never admit it, but they do. They come because their boyfriends can't give it to them like I can.' I had to scream at him to get him to stop telling me. He is a total liar. He knew what was at stake. The only person who could get him out of prison was Lorin and he did a job on you.

LORIN: His tears were real. He was ashamed he was having them. They were real.

MICK: Look, I believe what he said on that tape. I believe he didn't want to get hooked back into that stuff. I believe he fought it for a week. I believe he almost rang you, Lorin. But hell, what are we talking about here? He held off killing Donna for a *week*.

DEREK: Exactly.

MICK: I'm with you one hundred and fifty percent, Mr Milsom. I makes no difference at all. He's taken your girl's life and he's ruined mine, and I hate him and I hope he dies.

GAIL & CORAL: [*together*] Mick!

MICK: When they'd sentenced him and all those TV cameras were at the court, Mr Milsom, and they asked you how you felt and you said, 'I wish there was capital punishment'. I said to m'self, 'Yeah. Right on.' I think you've got a right to feel that way and you've got a right to say it.

BARBARA: Thank you, Mick. That really means a lot to me.

GAIL: You hate him that much, Mick. That you want him to die?

MICK: Yeah, I do.

GAIL: Have you forgotten how we grew up, Mick? In a concrete housing commission slum. The stink of uncollected garbage always in the air. Where I couldn't step outside the front door without being scared stiff I was going to be molested or bashed.

CORAL: Gail, it wasn't that bad.

GAIL: Mum, it was. And the place you're living in now isn't all that much better.

CORAL: It's a hell of a lot better.

MICK: [*to* GAIL] You won't be happy until you're living in a mansion in bloody Vaucluse.

GAIL: Mick, it was horrible.

CORAL: You always had food in your stomachs and clothes to wear.

GAIL: It was a nightmare.

CORAL: Gail!

GAIL: Mum, it wasn't your *fault!*

DEREK: So what are you saying here? Scott wasn't to blame? It was all due to the fact he wasn't brought up in the right suburb?

GAIL: You're very good with research that supports your stance, Derek. Why don't you read a bit on the other side as well? Weatherburn and Lind, 1998. Parental neglect is the single most important factor in creating criminal behaviour in children.

CORAL: I didn't neglect any of you.
GAIL: Ma, I'm not *blaming* you. You had no husband or partner. When you did get home you were exhausted. There were no family support programs of any kind.
CORAL: You weren't neglected.
GAIL: Scott ran wild. We never saw him. Out all night.
CORAL: I tried to keep him home at night. I tried.
GAIL: I know.
CORAL: I tried. He just laughed and went off.
GAIL: You had no help. Uncle Bob was useless.
BOB: I beg your bloody pardon?
GAIL: When Mum got you across to try and whip him into shape you'd just chuckle and say, 'Boys will be boys'.
BOB: What? I'm to blame for all this now?
GAIL: Well, you weren't much bloody help.
BOB: I had kids of my own.
GAIL: If a kid like Scott can roam free at any time of night, who do you think he's going to be roaming with, given we lived in the suburb with the highest crime rate in the city? If you read the Weatherburn figures, where we lived we were way out there on the graph in a class of our own. One in *three* kids over eleven, yes eleven, are out on our streets doing exactly what they like every night where we lived. Combine parental neglect with a high crime area and you've got an *epidemic* of young offenders. And that's exactly the word Weatherburn and Lind use. *Epidemic*. What kind of attitudes and values do you think Scott was going to pick up?
DEREK: Just be a little careful, Gail. That kind of rhetoric makes me really angry.
GAIL: You think an upbringing like we had has no effect whatsoever?
BOB: Gail, don't do this number again.
GAIL: You don't think—?
BOB: I can't hack that type of whingeing. I built up an equipment hire firm that employs fifty-five people and I started out just as poor as your mother. All you need to do is get off your arse and make an effort.
GAIL: Were you out on the streets at all hours when you were eleven? No, your father would've killed you.
CORAL: I didn't let him out on the streets. He just *went*.

BOB: Okay, Scott didn't have a dad, but I did my best with him. Too lenient in hindsight, but I did my best.
CORAL: Hah! First time he got into trouble, you dumped him.
BOB: I can't have someone dealing with my customers who's up on a rape charge.
CORAL: That first one was a date that went wrong. He didn't go to prison and if he'd still had his job with you—
BOB: You know how a business like mine works? Reputation. You make people happy with the service you provide and they come back to you next time.
CORAL: If you'd kept him on your payroll he'd've had something to lose. He was hit really bad when you dumped him. He got as bitter as hell.
BOB: I had to do what I had to do. Now can we get on with this and stop trying to blame it all on his damn upbringing.
DEREK: Thank God there's someone in this room who's not trying to find excuses.
BARBARA: I just get so sick of all these childhood sob stories. The truth is this is the nearest thing to a classless society on God's earth.
GAIL: Mrs Milsom, are you joking?
DEREK: It's true. In this country everyone gets a chance.
GAIL: A bit more research you might read, Derek. Bureau of Statistics. Top ten percent of the population has seventy percent of the wealth, bottom ten percent has one percent. And getting worse every day.
DEREK: So tell me how this killed my daughter, Gail?
GAIL: Contributed, Derek. Not killed, contributed. And I have told you, but I'll tell you again. Kids in our underclass suburbs with little to no parenting learn their values from the street. School sucks for them and, believe me, in those areas it does. They mightn't be academic, but they're not stupid. They know that the good life they see on the movies and television is never going to be for them. Not by any legitimate process. Add to that the fact that they're treated like shit—
BOB: Gail, come on.
GAIL: Bob, they're not blind. They know the job interview is over before it starts as soon as the employer sees their tats and hears their accents. They see the sneers on the faces of the rich kids at the K-Mart clothes they're wearing.

BOB: For God's sake, Gail. One of my best friends supplies jeans to K-Mart and they have to be made to the highest standards.
GAIL: If you've got energy, anger and no legitimate way out it's an explosive mix. The values they learn are that what you get in this life, you have to take.
BOB: Gail, this is bullshit.
GAIL: Okay, Uncle Bob. You've got the gift of the gab and a huge hunger for money so you made it. Not everyone's like you, and quite frankly thank God. Will you just try and stop swelling up with pride like a toad every time you open your mouth?
BOB: The worst money I ever spent was the money that helped you through university.
GAIL: My mother paid most. As usual you just came in at the end and grabbed all the credit.
BOB: That's gratitude for you.
GAIL: I'm grateful. I'm grateful.
DEREK: Gail, *exactly* how did childhood hardship turn your brother into a killer?
GAIL: Childhood poverty and neglect did not 'turn' my brother into a killer. But it most certainly *contributed*. To the anger, the nihilism, the sense that there's a world out there of things he can never have. Unless you take. And Scott took in the most horrible of all possible ways, and I hate what he did, but there were factors, and I can't cut him out of my life as if he were some sort of cancer.
BARBARA: Gail, there is no excuse for what he did. None. You and Mick had exactly the same upbringing.
GAIL: I didn't say *every* kid who's neglected is out on the streets. What I said was that in a single parent family where we lived, the *chances* of kids going wrong go up. Dramatically.
DEREK: God Almighty, Gail! We're not living in India where there's *real* poverty. This is one of the richest countries in the world.
GAIL: And one of the most unequal.
BARBARA: No one judges anyone by what suburb they come from in this country?
GAIL: Are you joking? Look what the media did to Scott's trial.
BARBARA: Just what did the media do?
GAIL: 'Savage Westie kid kills beautiful Eastern Suburbs middle-class girl'.

BARBARA: Did anyone ever say that? Even hint it?

GAIL: It was there. Don't worry it was there. Television crews everywhere every day. And you two would arrive with your entourage of Donna's private school friends and sit there in the court surrounded by them and stare at us with total hatred.

BARBARA: Donna's friends wanted to come. We didn't drag them there.

GAIL: The way you all behaved made me sick. And it made me feel more and more loyal to Scott despite what he did.

CORAL: Our family was suffering in our way, just as much as you were, but everyone was hating us a zillion times more.

GAIL: I can't sell Scott out like Mick and Bob. They've swallowed the media myth that this is a fair and just society like most people do.

BOB: Nobody's saying there isn't a rich and a poor, but—

GAIL: Even if Scott *did* have a sociopathic predisposition that doesn't mean he had to become what he became. Some of the most successful entrepreneurs in the world test through the roof on N Mach scales.

DEREK: Which are?

GAIL: The Machiavellian scale. The polite way of testing for sociopathy. The difference is that they had parents who had the time and money to make sure their ruthlessness was put to good use.

DEREK: So what do you want us to say, Gail? That we accept that our middle-class indifference to social justice caused all this? That we killed our own daughter?

GAIL: Derek, go and see how the other half *do* live. Fifty percent youth unemployed. Nothing to do but hang around the streets and wait until the local pushers eventually get them on heroin. Then there's only three options. Prison, OD or suicide. Some life.

DEREK: So tell me. Not in generalities, but in detail—how did *you* avoid that fate, Gail?

GAIL: Because I'm not Scott. I don't have a sociopathic predisposition and neither does Mick. But Scott did.

DEREK: So this tragedy had to happen.

GAIL: No, the tragedy didn't have to happen. It nearly *didn't* happen. Scott started working with Bob and he was doing really well.

BOB: You're determined to sheet this back to me.

GAIL: You said it yourself. 'He's going great guns. He'll run his own business one day.'

BOB: He was charged with rape. I couldn't keep him on. I just couldn't.
DEREK: Can we please get back to the reality? Whatever 'factors'—and of course there'll be factors—that contributed to what Scott became, men who've raped two or three times and who have violent sexual fantasies are lethal. They have to be either locked up long-term or given proven and effective therapy. Is that really too much to ask? I've lost a daughter that I loved more than anything in this world. Can any of you even *begin* to understand what we've been through?!

> DEREK *hangs his head in great distress, just managing to keep back the tears.*

JACK: Yes. Can we try and focus back on Donna?
GAIL: What more is there to say? What Scott did was appalling and it's screwed up the lives of your family and mine.
BARBARA: There's more *I* want to say.

> *There's a tense silence.*

[*To the* WILLIAMS *family*] I came here today to make you understand what your son put us through and I don't think you've even *started* to.

> *There's a tense silence.*

He's your brother, Gail, and he's your son, Coral, but you haven't *started* to understand what he put us through.
GAIL: We've heard a lot, Barbara.
BARBARA: You haven't *begun* to hear. What Scott did has not only robbed us of Donna's future. It's taken away her past. That's the worst thing. It's taken away her past.

> *There's a silence.*

My sister came over a while back and said to me that at least I had twenty wonderful years with Donna. I know she was trying to help, but I wanted to kill her. I literally wanted to claw her eyes out. I can't even open any photo album with Donna in it because I know there's a day, the tenth of August 1999, where it's going to end in indescribable terror, pain and worst of all, aloneness. Because I wasn't there for her. That's why Derek and I can't bear to stay together. Every time we look at each other we know there's that day in 1999 when it's all going to end in the most hideous way it could have, and neither of us was there for her. I'm sorry, but whatever the other 'factors' involved, and I don't deny there were other factors, we can't forgive your brother, ever. The pain he gave me will be with me every day until I die.

> *Tears start rolling down* BARBARA's *face.* DEREK *fights back tears and succeeds. He reaches out and hugs* BARBARA's *shoulder.* BARBARA's *speech has affected* GAIL, *however, and tears appear in her eyes.*

CORAL: [*quietly*] We know.

> *There's a silence.* BOB *squirms in his seat.*

BOB: The truth is this whole thing was goin' t'be a disaster right from the start. Gail's right. The only thing that was ever going to stop Scott was a father who came down hard on him. I warned Coral that Scott's dad was hopeless, but she went ahead and married him and he was gone before Mick was ever born.

CORAL: Which is why I asked you to help a bit.

BOB: And I did. And he *was* doing well working for me. But rape? I can't understand how any man could ever rape.

CORAL: Bob.

BOB: What?

CORAL: Nothin'.

BOB: What?

CORAL: You used to tell him how women were only good for one thing all the bloody time.

BOB: That was just a joke.

CORAL: You keep saying you knew Scott was bad right from the start—

BOB: He was.

CORAL: Well, you could've fooled me. You took him off to junior league so often when he was a kid he could've been your own son.

GAIL: 'Thank God we've got a little man in the family' you kept saying. 'I was cursed with three daughters.'

BOB: I was jokin'.

GAIL: Didn't make me laugh.

BOB: What does?

CORAL: You used to tell Scott he could do anything. Praise him to the skies. Brag about the crazy tackles he'd make on boys twice his size. 'That boy is fearless', you used to yell. 'Totally fearless'.

BOB: He *was* the gutsiest little football player I ever saw. Crazy.
CORAL: So just when was it you got this heavy feeling he was headed for disaster? All I ever remember was you cheerin' him on. If there was anyone laughing *really* loud when Scott told his stories it was you!
BOB: A man can't help liking a kid with no fear, but I could still see the way he was goin' to turn out.
CORAL: Gail's right. You never did *nothing* to haul him into line. Ever.
BOB: He wasn't my kid.
GAIL: Well, none of us would've known. Because that's the way you treated him.
CORAL: And the one time he really needed you—when he got into trouble about that first girl—you dropped him. Like he didn't exist. Sacked him from his job when I was in hospital and there wasn't a dollar in the house. You can all call Scott a monster, but he went out and came home with the hundred and fifty dollars that got us through. And he didn' rob anyone to get it. He sold the one thing that was really precious to him. His CD collection. There was another side to my boy and you used to love that side of him, Bob, whether you want t'remember it or not.

There's a silence. JACK *keeps looking at* BOB.

JACK: Do you think maybe he did need you after that first rape charge, Bob?
BOB: For God's sake, I had to think of my business.
CORAL: Your business. If we heard you braggin' about that damn business of yours one more time I would've told you to shove it. Right at that time Scott needed you to yell at him and tell him he'd let you down, you dump him. If there was one man in the world he respected it was you.
JACK: Bob, has Coral got a point?
BOB: I did what I could.

BOB *stares ahead defiantly. There's a short silence.*

CORAL: Bob won't tell you but there was a better side to Scott. I've just been too bloody scared to say it. He didn't just tell stories about beating people up. He could take off anyone he ever met. He could do Bob till the tears were streamin' down our face. And if Gail had've ever caught him doing Gail, well! He could've been an actor.

He could've been a footballer and he could've run a business just as well as his uncle. We've all heard how wonderful Donna was, and I'm sure she was, but my boy wasn't a monster till near the end and he could've been stopped. We've got one screwed-up boy and he's made your life hell, but I guess the real reason I wanted to come here tonight is to tell you he's made our lives hell too.

MICK: Mum cries herself t'sleep every night.

CORAL: I don't know your pain like you do, but I know pain.

BOB: And I sure don't feel great either.

CORAL: Barbara, you don't have to teach me about pain.

GAIL: Barbara, just because I'm trying to defend Scott, doesn't mean I approve of what he did. [*Pointing to the photo of Donna*] It's just horrible to look at her and think what she went through. Horrible. And it's awful to have to look in the eyes of my brother and know that he did it. I've screamed at him in jail.

CORAL: The guards had to drag her out.

GAIL: And I'm shocked at the pathetic apology he gave.

DEREK: He could apologise till doomsday and it would still do no good! You could all apologise till doomsday and it would do no good.

GAIL: So why are we here? If no amount of us saying we're sorry is going to ease the hate in your heart, then why are we here?

JACK: Derek?

DEREK: I know now why you're here. To see if we'll help you get your son into protective custody. Unbelievable!

CORAL: It was just a thought I had and it was stupid.

DEREK: Yeah, it was. Really, really stupid. And, Coral, I don't care how much pain you have. The more the better. And the day I hear that your boy has been stabbed to death in prison I'll open champagne and celebrate.

GAIL: Ma, let's go. There's no point.

DEREK: Of course there's no point. There's never been a point. There never will be a point. Your mother got herself married to a no-hoper, had kids she couldn't cope with and put Barbara and I into a living nightmare.

CORAL: [*angrily*] Yeah, I did. And if I could wind back the clock, would I do it again? Probably. The thing I *did* get out've marrying that no-hoper was two kids I'm bloody proud of. Gail who battled on through everything and got where she is today and Mick who'd never hurt a fly. I couldn't want those two to never have been born! If you don't even want to hear that we're in pain too then there is no bloody point.

There's a tense silence.

JACK: Do you all think there is no further point?

GAIL: Doesn't seem to be. Derek's just too full of hate to hear anything we say.

JACK: Is that true, Derek?

DEREK: Their pain? We've been brought here to listen to *their* pain? Unbelievable.

JACK: You think it's unbelievable, Barbara?

BARBARA *is silent.*

Are we all agreed there's no further point to this?

LORIN: I've always doubted there would be.

There's a silence.

JACK: Nobody's leaving.

There's another silence.

DEREK: [*to* JACK] Don't *you* think it's unbelievable? That they want *us* to listen to *their* pain?

JACK: Do you think they *are* feeling pain?

DEREK: I don't care. I absolutely do not care.

BARBARA: Derek.

DEREK: What?

BARBARA: You don't need…

DEREK: What? Need what?

BARBARA: I understand Coral's pain.

DEREK: It's not what we're here for.

BARBARA: What are we here for?

DEREK: To make *them* feel pain.

CORAL: We have. And hate.

DEREK: What do you expect?

CORAL: Maybe that you'd finally believe we really are sorry.

DEREK: Sorry? Sorry's too damn easy.

BARBARA: Derek.

DEREK: What good is sorry? A million 'sorries' aren't going to bring her back.
JACK: Do you think there's no further point to this, Barbara?
BARBARA: If there is, Derek won't see it.
DEREK: Barbara.
BARBARA: It's true.
DEREK: What point is there to being here? What?
BARBARA: [*angrily*] There *are* other people in pain in this room beside you. Get out of your own head and start to listen!

There's a silence.

[*Quietly*] Derek, there are other people in pain.

There's a silence. GAIL *shifts uncomfortably in her chair.*

JACK: Gail? Is there anything that you think could move us forward.
GAIL: I'd just like to say how sad it made me to hear what Barbara said. That she's been robbed of Donna's past. It's hard enough for me to cope with the fact my brother took away Donna's future, but if he's taken her past too, that's… awful. Really awful.

BARBARA *looks away, tears in her eyes.*

I really wish she could open up those albums again.
CORAL: So do I.

There's a brief silence.

[*To* BARBARA] Can you talk about her, or is that too hard too?
BARBARA: No, talking is fine. I *wanted* to talk about her. All the time.
DEREK: You talked too much.
BARBARA: People didn't want to listen.

There's a silence.

Derek wouldn't listen either.
DEREK: Talking about her just upset you.
BARBARA: No, it upset you.

There's a silence.

JACK: Tell us about her, Barbara.
DEREK: No!
JACK: I think people might like to hear.
CORAL: I'd like to hear.

DEREK: No.

There's a silence. BARBARA *looks at* CORAL *and nods.*

BARBARA: When she was thirteen, she wanted her birthday party at this particular restaurant.

DEREK: How the hell can you talk about Donna to *them?*

BARBARA: [*angrily*] Because they want to listen! [*To* GAIL] It had to be this restaurant and no other. She was always very definite about what she wanted. [*She reflects and smiles.*] She knew exactly who she wanted invited.

DEREK: Barbara, this is sick. They're the last people who should hear.

BARBARA: [*ignoring him*] We did everything she asked. Twenty-eight friends. Went through the menu with her. Got every detail right. And it was wonderful. I was taking far too many photos like I always do—but to hell with it, I think, and use up two rolls, three. There's so much laughter. Donna just *loved* being with friends. Loved the jokes. The shared things. And the wonderful thing for me about that day is that I'm allowed to see it all. Allowed to be there while Donna is totally, totally happy. I've got tears in my eyes and can hardly take the photos. Then came our surprise. We'd arranged a magician. The best. The most expensive. But the minute he appears Donna's eyes go black with rage. [*She smiles and nods her head.*] And I think, 'Uh-oh. Bad move.' And Donna sits there stony-faced as the magician does his routine. And he's good. Really good. And funny. [*Thinking*] Well, the humour was a little corny. But still funny. But Donna didn't think so. That's for sure. Those eyes. She just gave me one furious glance and I knew we were in for it. When we got home she just flounced off to her room, stayed there for an hour, then came down and let us have it.

She smiles, remembering it.

[*Imitating her daughter*] 'You ruined it. Totally ruined it. How could you ever think we'd like that pathetic guy and his pathetic tricks?' Her friends actually loved it. I could tell, but not according to our daughter. [*She imitates her again.*] 'Magicians are for babies. Do you know what's happening now? Do you? Do you? All my friends are calling around saying, "What about that magician? Does Donna really think we go for that sort of stuff? Doesn't she know that magicians are just sooo uncool.'" So I said that if her friends were going to drop her because of that then they're friends who weren't worth having. Which of course made things worse. [*She pauses for a second or two, remembering.*] We learned our lesson. We never did anything again without checking it out with her. The truth was she was a regular little control freak.

DEREK: The magician was pathetic. She was right to be mad.

BARBARA: She could twist Derek round her little finger.

DEREK: Will you stop this?

BARBARA: In Derek's eyes she could do no wrong. But mothers know better. She was a regular little control freak.

CORAL: So's Gail. Remember the roller blades?

BOB: When I got the wrong brand?

GAIL: Mum, we're talking about Donna.

CORAL: Sorry.

BARBARA: No, no.

CORAL: When you were talking about her she seemed so real.

BARBARA: It's funny that. I can talk about her. I could happily talk about her all day, but I just can't look at the photos. Why would that be?

CORAL: When you see a photo it brings so much more back.

BARBARA: No, I don't think that's it. When I tell a story like that I can see her in my mind's eye just as vividly as any photo. And I can look at that photo of Donna there. [*She points.*] I just can't open those albums.

LORIN: Maybe it's because the photos are in sequence. Leading to—

BARBARA: Yes. Yes of course. Leading to—

GAIL: Take the photos out of the albums. Shuffle them round.

BARBARA: [*looking at* GAIL] So I never know what's coming next? You know something? I think that might work.

GAIL: You could always talk about her. So it must be the sequence thing.

BARBARA: [*nodding*] Right from the start. I wanted to talk about her all the time.

LORIN: People do.

BARBARA: But Derek's right. No one wanted to listen. The more I wanted to talk, the more no one wanted to listen. They were embarrassed. 'Try and forget', they'd say, 'Put it out of your mind. You've got to get on with your life.'

DEREK: You talked about her too much.
BARBARA: I had to.
DEREK: You were driving our friends away.
BARBARA: Yeah, I was. I did. I have.
LORIN: People don't want to hear. They feel guilty.
BARBARA: Guilty?
LORIN: That their children are still alive. They can't stop themselves thinking that if someone had to die, they're glad it was your daughter and not theirs.

   BARBARA *nods.*

It's normal. People can't stop themselves feeling that way. But they still should listen. People don't realise that they should listen. It's the best thing they can do for you.

   There's a pause.

GAIL: [*to* BARBARA] I bet she forgave you. For the magician.
BARBARA: [*nodding*] She could never maintain the rage for very long. There was another time—
DEREK: Barbara that's enough. We've heard enough!
BARBARA: There was another time—
DEREK: Barbara!
BARBARA: [*angrily*] You've spent a year looking up facts and figures and statistics so now you think you *own* our daughter's death. Well you don't. She was my daughter. I bore her. Stop trying to manage my grief!

   There's a brief silence.

I'd been sitting with her in the hospital, holding her hand what—ten minutes? Twenty minutes? And you told me that that was enough. That was enough!
DEREK: She was dead.
BARBARA: You said, 'Come on. It won't do any good to stay with her too long.'
DEREK: You'd been with her an hour.
BARBARA: And I just got up and meekly did what I was told. And I've been angry with you and myself ever since.
DEREK: I just thought—
BARBARA: I knew how long I wanted to spend with my daughter. You had no right to control that!

DEREK: I'm sorry. I just thought…

He trails off into silence. BARBARA *turns back to* LORIN, CORAL *and* GAIL.

BARBARA: There was another time when she came down one morning and looked at the kitchen and said, 'This kitchen sucks. You painted it the wrong colour.' So I said, 'All right, Miss Know-It-All, what colour should it be?' 'Daffodil Yellow', she said. 'Well', I said 'I'll buy the paint if you do the painting'. I knew of course that she's never done any painting in her life. But she knew I was calling her bluff and she never backed down from a challenge, so there she was on Saturday, in big work overalls, turning our kitchen Daffodil Yellow.

DEREK: And she looked—

He stops.

BARBARA: [*to* DEREK] Say it. Talk about her.

DEREK: She looked at it when she'd finished and said, 'I was wrong'.

From left: Robert Coleby as Derek, Diane Craig as Barbara, Sandy Gore as Lorin, Geoff Cartwright as Jack, Bianca Rowe as Gail and Deborah Kennedy as Coral in the 2001 Ensemble Theatre production in Sydney. (Photo: Robert McFarlane)

BARBARA: It's still Daffodil Yellow.

DEREK: We all got used to it.

BARBARA: But anyone that's never seen it before just looks, and we know they're thinking, 'Are they colourblind?'. And when Donna was there and saw them looking she'd just smile at me.

DEREK: She was honest enough to admit she was wrong, but too lazy to fix it.

CORAL: Gail never did a thing around the house. 'I'm studying!' Like is this the only person in the history of the world that ever went to uni?

GAIL: Mum, we're not talking about me.

BARBARA: That's fine.

JACK: Barbara, Derek, thank you for telling us those stories.

BARBARA: I didn't do it to make anyone feel guilty—

CORAL: We know.

BARBARA: I just want people to know how she was.

There's a silence.

LORIN: Barbara, I haven't told the whole truth.

There's a silence.

The night before I gave testimony I went over all Scott's test scores again. His Hare, his MMPI, and I remember thinking, 'This is a text book sociopath. This is a *dangerous* young man.' But I saw him again in the morning and...

JACK: And?

LORIN: He could be charming. God knows he could be charming. And funny. He knew I'd been having a hard time with the prison governor. A troglodyte if ever there was one. And he imitated him brilliantly. Brought tears to my eyes.

CORAL: I even used to laugh when he did me.

DEREK: What are you saying, Lorin?

LORIN: I should have known what he was doing. I did know what he was doing.

DEREK: You lost all your objectivity because he charmed you?

LORIN: I lost my objectivity. For whatever reason.

DEREK: You're paid to be objective. You're paid to be professional!

BARBARA: Lorin, you don't forget the basics of your craft because someone makes you laugh.

LORIN: No you don't.

There's a silence.

BARBARA: What are you saying? You were infatuated with him? A rapist and killer?

LORIN: I don't know what I was. All I know is that I wanted to believe in him. More than I should've.

BARBARA: Sounds suspiciously like infatuation to me.

LORIN: Call it what you like.

DEREK: Infatuated?

LORIN: Yes probably. And I shouldn't've been. And I've ruined your life. What do you want me to do? What *exactly* do you want me to do? Kill myself? I've felt badly enough about this to just about contemplate it. I've driven my partner away for good because he couldn't stand me obsessing about it any longer. I could have stopped this tragedy, but I didn't.

There's another total silence.

I'm on compassionate stress leave now, but I won't be going back. Don't worry, Jack, it wasn't this conference. I'd decided that weeks ago. I can't ever risk this happening again. I'm sorry. To all of you.

There's another silence.

MICK: [*to* LORIN] You're not the only one to blame.

They look at him.

I could've saved your daughter, Mrs Milsom. I knew she was goin' t'get raped. I saw it building up day after day. I told my brother I'd kill him if he tried it, but he's not scared of me. He's not scared of anyone. I've seen him pick fights with guys twice his size and get the shit beaten out of him and go back a few days later and do it again. I went up to your daughter and I was goin' t'say, 'See that guy over there. Take every bloody precaution. He's raped two women already and he's looking at you.' And then she would've phoned you and then you would've had her guarded or had her live back home and she'd still be alive. But when I said, 'Excuse me, can we talk?', she looked at me, and turned on her heel. It was like 'Don't come near *me*, scum'.

DEREK: She wouldn't've reacted that way.

MICK: She did.
DEREK: She was probably just being cautious.
MICK: I had the wrong kind of accent and the wrong clothes. Simple as that.
DEREK: She wasn't like that.
MICK: I know I still should have told her, but when I get treated like that it pisses me off, so I said to myself, 'Fuck you, get yourself raped, you stuck-up bitch'.
DEREK: You callous little shit!
MICK: I never thought he'd kill her.
DEREK: [*angrily*] You *wanted* her to be raped? Out of sheer spite? Here you are presenting yourself as better than your brother, and you know what? You're worse. Ten times worse. He was in the grip of a compulsion. A sick, sick compulsion, but what were you in the grip of, what? Spite. Nothing more than spite. You wanted her to be raped because she turned away? Because she was understandably a little cautious.
MICK: It wasn't that, she just thought I was shit.
DEREK: Barbara, support me. You know damn well the last thing our daughter was was a snob.
MICK: Sorry. I've seen that look a thousand times. 'Who does this guy think he is, trying to hit on *me?*'
DEREK: Barbara, tell him. Our daughter was not a snob.

There's a silence.

BARBARA: Derek, our daughter could be a *horrible* little snob.
DEREK: For that she deserves to die?
MICK: Of course she didn't. She deserved to be warned. And I let my anger get the better of me. I'm really sorry. I am.
DEREK: [*in a fury*] I've had all these 'sorries'. Up to the neck. You knew your brother was a dangerous animal but for the sake of an extra step or two on your part, my daughter is dead.
BOB: If you could make Scott die ten times over it still wouldn't be good enough for you, would it? What do you bloody want? Our whole family dead? Would that make you feel better?

There's a silence.

There's thousands of things that could've happened that could've changed things, Derek. If you go down that road too far you go mad. Yeah sure, I shouldn't've fired him after that first rape charge. I was thinkin' of my wallet, not him. And there's other things keep *me* awake at night too.

JACK: Such as?

BOB: Thinkin' what turned him onto violent sex in the first place.

JACK: Do you have any thoughts on that, Bob?

BOB: Yes. And I hope to hell they're not right because I miss what that kid could've been. Sure he had no guilt, but you have to love a little kid that'll take risks and talk his way out've anything. Let's face it. Most of the millionaires in this country are full-on sociopaths.

GAIL: Like I said before. If you've been born to a privileged background, having no fear and no guilt can be very profitable.

JACK: The violent sex? Bob?

BOB: Okay. His first few girlfriends wouldn't do it and I told him…

JACK: What?

BOB: That some girls say no when they really mean yes. It's just a thing you say.

CORAL: It's a thing no man should say. Especially not when a kid worships him.

BOB: A few months later he said something to me when we're driving some equipment out to a customer. But I'm thinking business and I only half hear it. And I just say, 'yeah'. And at the end of the day I think, 'What? *What* did he say?' And it comes back to me jus' as if it's tape recorded in my brain. 'It's more fun when they struggle.' And I think, 'Shit, I've got to talk to this kid', but of course business, embarrassment—whatever. I didn't. So. Derek. I guess I'm one of Gail's 'factors'. Just like all the rest of this family. Get a gun and shoot us.

DEREK: That's not going to bring her back.

MICK: Nothin's going to bring her back, Mr Milsom. Or bring back my best mate Jimmy Griffiths. Knifed to death in Pitt Street by a junkie 'cause he only had seven dollars on him. What would've kept him alive? Twenty dollars, the price of a fix. A human life for thirteen dollars. That's pretty scary shit. Can't sleep at nights thinking 'bout it. His dad Neil is my boss at the supermarket. And Neil seemed okay. Copin' with it all. But two days back I went out to the dispatch bay, and there he was crouched over the bushes dry retching and crying like a baby. Frankly, workin' out what life's about is beyond me. It's a total mystery. All I can do from here on in is keep goin'. There's got to be some good along with all this shit eventually.

CORAL: Some people sail through an' never experience a day's misery in their life. And don't I jus' hate 'em. But some people get the worst. It's like a bloody lottery. Yeah, I worked long hours and yeah, I was exhausted, but I still could've stood up and screamed at him and stopped trying to find excuses for everything he did. A blind fool could've seen where he was headed and I should've tried to plant m'self square in his path and said 'no'. Your kids are the scariest bloody lottery of all. My number came up and I got a hell of a tough one, an' I tried, but I should've tried harder. Don't know whether it would've done much good but I should've tried. If there's anything I can do to make life easier for you both, I'll do it. I mean it. I really do. I mean it.

BARBARA: Thank you.

GAIL: Barbara, just so you know, I'm never, ever going to be able to cope with what my brother did. Never. I grew up with only a thin bit of plaster separating my room from his, and that gives me nightmares of my own and I don't have to tell you what those nightmares are, but they're truly horrible. But I can't just cut my brother out of my life.

    BARBARA *nods*.

If there was anything I could do to help, like Mum, I'd do it too. I don't know what, but I'd do it.

    The tears are now streaming out of her eyes. BARBARA *goes and picks up the photo of Donna and returns to her seat and looks down at it. There's a silence.*

JACK: Barbara, is there anything else you'd like to say?

BARBARA: Yes. [*She looks down at the photo again.*] Maybe if any of you believe in God… you could pray for her. In your own time. In your own way.

CORAL: I will.

    DEREK *shifts uncomfortably.*

JACK: Derek. Is there anything you want to say?

    DEREK *nods*.

DEREK: She was followed once before. About six months before she... I promised I would get her one of those panic buttons. Little pendants you can hang around your neck. They look like a real necklace. You press and it's radio relayed and it goes straight to a patrolling security firm. But I didn't do it, did I? I was too busy with my bloody useless career. She wanted her boyfriend to move in with her and I told her I didn't think she should make that sort of commitment just yet. 'Give yourself some freedom. Give yourself some time', that's what I said. My real objection? He was a musician in a rock band. And he hadn't been to a private school and he hadn't been to university. If there's a bit of the snob in our daughter then I guess she got it from me.

There's a silence.

I knew she was at risk living alone in that area. Barbara kept asking me if I'd arranged for that panic button, and I kept getting irritated and saying, 'I'll do it soon'.

DEREK *still has tears rolling down his face. There's a silence.*

JACK: Is there anything else anyone would like to say?

CORAL: I know it wasn't on the agenda, but if Scott isn't granted protective custody he's as good as dead.

DEREK: [*irritated*] If he's in real danger they'll grant it.

GAIL: That's not how jails work, Derek.

CORAL: Our lawyer says there's still no certainty the application'll be granted even if you two did sign. But it'd help. A lot.

DEREK: Coral, I know you're a decent human being. I know the dice fell the wrong way for you. But just don't ask me to do that. There are boundaries to compassion and your boy's crossed them. If I signed I'd feel like I'd betrayed my daughter. Don't you see that?

BARBARA: Scott's going to spend the rest of his life in prison, Derek. Isn't that enough?

DEREK: You're going to sign? Is that what you're saying?

BARBARA: If Scott *is* killed I'm not sure I'd sleep easily.

DEREK: Why not, for God's sake?

BARBARA: Because Coral's a mother, just like I am.

DEREK: You'd be betraying Donna.

BARBARA: She's dead, Derek.

GAIL: Barbara, Derek won't change.
DEREK: [*pointing at* MICK] Your own brother wants him dead! How can you *possibly* expect forgiveness out of me? Your own brother wants him dead.
MICK: [*shaking his head*] No. Not because I don't hate him. Because it'd finish Mum.
CORAL: [*angrily*] You don't want him dead because he's your *brother!*
MICK: [*shaking his head*] I don't want him dead 'cause of you.
BARBARA: I'm sorry, Derek, but I feel that way too.
DEREK: You're going to sign?
BARBARA: Yes I am.
CORAL: Bless you, Barbara. Bless you. He's bad, always was, but he's my son.
DEREK: Sorry. I can't.

> *There's a pause. The silence grows. The pressure on* DEREK *grows.*

I can't. Not here. Not now.

> *There's a pause.*

JACK: Anything else anyone wants to say?
GAIL: Derek, I know how upset you are and I don't want to rub salt into the wounds, but this is going to happen again and again as long as there are families who grow up like we did and, Mum, I'm *not* pointing the finger at you. I'm pointing the finger at governments that do everything they can to help the rich get richer and to ghettoise the poor, and who—
BOB: Gail, get off the bloody soapbox.
GAIL: —and who cut social services and education to the bone so there's no family support systems and no community services of any kind.
BOB: Gail!
GAIL: Executives granting themselves huge bonuses so they can fly around in their own private jets are the very same ones who bray loudest for 'law and order'. The only law *they* obey is the law of greed.
BOB: Gail!
GAIL: All done, Uncle Bob. But you'll hear it again.
BOB: Don't I know it.
JACK: No one else?

Silence.

Okay, but don't feel you have to go. Talk to each other as long as you like.

They all look at each other. Some of them get out of their seats but they all want to stay and talk. We hear some of the talk as the lights begin to fade.

BARBARA: [*to* GAIL] I'm going to try that thing. Mixing the photos up. Where are you living?

GAIL: Canberra.

BARBARA: You must miss her.

CORAL: Sure, but in one way it's a blessing. She and Mick [*shaking her head*] … won't ever get rid of the violence in the world if those two are in the same house.

BARBARA: What are you doing in Canberra, Gail?

GAIL: Policy adviser to a shadow minister.

CORAL: God help those MPs.

GAIL: I'm on a plane back there in the morning.

BOB: Thank you, Lord.

BARBARA: Coral, thank you for setting this up. We'll share the cost.

CORAL: Oh no you bloody well won't.

BARBARA: Thank you.

LORIN *gets up out of her seat.*

LORIN: Thank you, Jack.

JACK: Thank *you*. I know it was hard.

LORIN: I'm never going to be a total convert. But—I am glad I was here.

She leaves.

CORAL: [*to* DEREK] I understand how you feel, Derek. But if you could find it in your heart to help, I'd be so grateful.

DEREK *nods. The* WILLIAMS *family exits.* BARBARA *stays behind waiting for* DEREK *who is still sitting.*

DEREK: [*to* BARBARA *and* JACK] I don't think I can. I just don't think I can.

JACK: You don't have to decide now.

BARBARA: [*to* JACK, *shaking her head*] You do this for a living?

JACK: [*smiling*] They're not *all* as tough as today. [*To* DEREK] I hope you got something out of this, Derek?

DEREK: [*nodding*] There's a weight of some kind been lifted.
JACK: Good.

> DEREK *finally gets up and moves towards* BARBARA *who has her hand held out for him. They exit.* JACK *stands there watching them go.*

THE END

Charitable Intent

From left: Margaret Mills as Stella, Denis Moore as Brian, Vivienne Walshe as Bryony and Michael Fry as Jack in the 2001 La Mama production in Melbourne. (Photo: David van Royen)

Charitable Intent was first performed at the La Mama Theatre, Melbourne, as part of the 2001 Melbourne Festival, on 10 October 2001, with the following cast:

JACK MANNING	Michael Fry
TAMSYN	Trudy Hellier
CASSIE	Tammy McCarthy
STELLA	Margaret Mills
BRIAN	Denis Moore
AMANDA	Carole Patullo
GIULIA	Maria Theodorakis
BRYONY	Vivienne Walshe

Director, Tom Gutteridge
Designer, Tanja Beer
Lighting Design and Operation, Richard Dinnen
Stage Manager, Jo Leishman

CHARACTERS

JACK MANNING, community conference convenor
TAMSYN, early 30s
CASSIE, mid-20s
STELLA, early 50s
BRIAN, early 50s
AMANDA, mid-40s
GIULIA, mid-20s
BRYONY, mid-30s

A meeting room in the headquarters of a large national charitable organisation. JACK MANNING, *forty-ish, is setting up eight chairs in a horseshoe formation facing out towards the audience. There is nothing much other than a hot water urn and tea and coffee making facilities and a small table on which there is a plate of biscuits.* AMANDA, *mid-forties, and* STELLA, *early fifties, enter.* AMANDA *is overweight and is dressed in unfashionable drab clothing and looks worried and anxious.* STELLA *is more smartly dressed and looks more angry than anxious.* JACK *looks up and smiles.*

JACK: Hi Amanda. Hi Stella. First here.
STELLA: I hope this sorts out this mess one way or another.
JACK: That's what we're here for.
AMANDA: I don't even know if I care anymore.
STELLA: I care.

> BRIAN *enters. He's in his early fifties wearing an expensive business suit and with the kind of set look on his face that declares that life is an unending battle against inefficiency and complacency.*

JACK: Brian. Thanks for coming.

> BRIAN *looks askance at* AMANDA *and* STELLA *who nod greetings, which he perfunctorily returns.*

BRIAN: Things can't go on as they are.
JACK: So it seems.
BRIAN: I hope this doesn't end up as yet another exercise in employer bashing.
JACK: That's not what it's intended to do.
BRIAN: [*looking at* AMANDA *and* STELLA] There seems to be a lingering feeling in some quarters that charitable organisations shouldn't be efficient, businesslike and accountable. It's an attitude I don't share.
JACK: So you said.
BRIAN: We're attracting millions of dollars in donations from a public that expect those dollars to be used wisely and efficiently and effectively.
JACK: They do. Help yourselves to coffee or tea.

BRIAN *nods and helps himself to a coffee.*

BRIAN: I just hope this isn't going to drag on too long. In my other life I've got a company to run.

JACK: These things tend to be a bit unpredictable, but I'm aware that everyone has time pressures.

TAMSYN, *early thirties,* CASSIE, *mid-twenties, and* GIULIA, *mid-twenties enter together. They're all attractive, slim and very well-groomed.*

Tamsyn, Cassie, Giulia. Thank you for coming. Help yourself to coffee or tea.

TAMSYN, CASSIE *and* GIULIA *smile warmly at* BRIAN, *who nods back, and nod evasively at* AMANDA *and* STELLA, *who nod back.*

BRIAN: [*to the three of them*] You're all looking very smart.

ALL THREE: Thank you.

BRIAN: Beautiful morning out there.

GIULIA: It really is.

CASSIE: You're really in the news *this* week, Brian.

BRIAN: I wish the financial journalists would just leave me alone.

CASSIE: It's a huge merger.

BRIAN: It hasn't happened yet, and I never count my chickens until they're hatched, grown and laying themselves.

CASSIE: It'll be a great feather in your cap if it *does* all happen.

BRIAN: The financial pages are carrying on as if it's a stroke of genius. The truth is that it's a move that was staring anyone in the face if they'd cared to look.

GIULIA: Yes, but you were the one who *did* look.

BRIAN: [*pleased at the flattery, despite himself*] All I can say is that that doesn't say much for my competitors.

BRYONY *enters. She's mid-thirties, impeccably dressed in a power suit and conveys an air of purpose and direction overlaid with an icy calmness. She wears a fixed false smile which hardly ever leaves her face.*

BRYONY: Sorry if I'm late.

JACK: You're not.

BRYONY: I had a string of calls, but I've turned my mobile off.

JACK: Thank you.

BRYONY: Brian. You really are the man of the moment. I'm amazed you've got the time to bother about our little problems.
BRIAN: I'm the Chair of your Board and I take that seriously.
BRYONY: Thank you. Many wouldn't.
BRYONY: [*nodding*] Giulia, Cassie, Tamsyn. I'm sorry this has dragged you away from your work. I just hope it's for good reason.
JACK: I hope so too.

BRYONY *nods formally at* STELLA *and* AMANDA.

BRYONY: I have to say, Brian, that I don't really see the need for this exercise. I *am* the Chief Executive Officer and I *am* perfectly capable of dealing with these sort of problems.
BRIAN: Personally I agree. But certain Board members felt that the levels of conflict you're experiencing might be best addressed by a workplace conference. I really appreciate your co-operation.
BRYONY: [*to* JACK] I hope it doesn't drag on. I'm not running an organisation on the scale of Brian's, but we do distribute over a hundred and seventy million dollars worth of charitable aid and that's what I'd rather be doing than this.
JACK: The conference might help you to do it more effectively, Bryony. At least that's the plan.
BRYONY: Can we get on with it then?
JACK: Absolutely.
BRYONY: [*looking at* AMANDA *and* STELLA] I have to issue one warning. If I'm subjected to unwarranted abuse of the sort that's become all too commonplace in this organisation, then I'm leaving.
JACK: I'm sure there'll be some strong words said, but try and hang in there.
BRIAN: I have to say I share Bryony's feelings. No CEO should be subjected to unwarranted attack from their staff.
JACK: Brian, Bryony isn't here today as a CEO and you're not here as Chair of the Board. Hopefully we're here as eight people whose feelings and ideas are listened to equally.
BRYONY: I don't want to be part of a process that generates ill will.
JACK: It seems like there's a lot of ill will around already, Bryony. All right. Let's get started. Amanda and Stella, if you can sit on this side of me here. [*He indicates.*] And Tamsyn next to me, then Cassie, Giulia, Brian and Bryony.

They settle themselves. There's a tense silence.

I've spoken to you all individually and you all are well aware of the reason you're here. It's obvious from what I've heard that the workplace atmosphere has become, in the words of almost all of you, 'poisonous'. I'll just take a second to explain again the rationale behind a workplace conference such as this. In some workplace situations there's a disagreement about facts, but people don't necessarily have negative feelings about each other. That's just a dispute. In this case however people do feel negatively about each other so we have a full-on conflict which is causing most of you distress, and affecting the efficiency of the whole organisation. Conflicts like this often arise out of misperceptions. We often attribute to other people far worse motives than they actually had. It seems to be a human failing. If we're frank and honest with each other today, we might just be able to unravel the causes of what's happened around here, and get things back to normal.

BRIAN: That sounds all very hopeful, but what if the bad feelings *aren't* due just to 'misunderstandings'?

JACK: That'd mean that the negative feelings around here have some real basis and then that becomes a problem for you and your board. Either way there'll be some clarification of what exactly is going on.

BRYONY: I know already what's going on.

JACK: From your perspective, Byrony. Another human failing is that we always tend to see things from our perspective. *Our* version of history is always slanted our way.

BRYONY: It's my job to see the picture from all perspectives.

JACK: And I'm sure that's exactly what you've tried to do, but hey, none of us are perfect. Okay, here's my understanding of the situation to make sure I've got it right. 'Enabling and Caring' is a long-established charitable organisation, collecting public donations for a range of different programs which you provide and oversee. These include youth services, disabled services and sheltered workshops, suicide prevention services, drug counselling, detox, emergency accommodation, family crisis intervention and so on. Two and a half years ago your CEO Alan Twomey retired after long service and the Board appointed Bryony to replace him. Shortly after Bryony took over she appointed Giulia as head of Public Relations and

Marketing, a role that Amanda had performed by default up to then, as Amanda's job is actually to head up Program Management. Shortly after Giulia's appointment, the workplace atmosphere started to deteriorate and has since got progressively worse.

GIULIA: I hope there's no inference there that I'm the cause of all our problems.

BRYONY: That's what it sounded like.

JACK: If it did, I'm very sorry. I was just trying to establish the chronology.

GIULIA: I'm not denying that my appointment was the cause of the onset of all this, but I am denying that I caused it.

AMANDA: I know I've been accused of having my nose put out of joint by Giulia's appointment—

BRYONY: By whom?

AMANDA: By you.

BRYONY: I'm sorry. That's not true at all.

AMANDA: Well whatever. All I'm saying is that if it was said, it wasn't true. When Bryony first took over I was frank and told her I'd had no formal training in PR and marketing and that any successes I'd had were due more to good luck than good management.

STELLA: Rubbish. You got on really well with the media and they all liked you.

GIULIA: Meaning that they don't like me?

STELLA: Amanda was a natural. She didn't need training.

GIULIA: Meaning that I'm not? I'm not a natural?

STELLA: If we're being frank, you can be a little too pushy.

GIULIA: Well 'hello', Stella. The world doesn't come to you these days. You have to go to it.

AMANDA: Look, I'm not trying to say I was any better or worse than Giulia. The truth is I was relieved when she was appointed because my workload was getting out of hand.

BRYONY: Which I perceived immediately, and which is why I brought Giulia in.

JACK: And you felt that Amanda accepted this?

BRYONY: She told me she was relieved, but it does seem that a new atmosphere developed around the place shortly afterwards. An atmosphere I've characterised as the 'culture of resistance'.

JACK: Resistance to?

BRYONY: New ideas. New ways of doing things.

STELLA: No one objected to Giulia per se. It's what you and she started *doing* we had reservations about.

BRYONY: What we did was bring a fresh and vigorous approach to the whole organisation.

JACK: What was the essence of this new approach, Bryony?

BRYONY: I'd come to E and C with considerable experience in other charitable organisations and I felt it was essential we didn't fall behind. And I have to say I did sense an air of—complacency's perhaps not the right word—

JACK: What is?

BRYONY: An organisation that was... set in its ways. I was aware of course of what a fine job Amanda and Stella had done over the years and I made sure I praised that work and gave credit for it, but my past experience told me that the fight for the charity dollar is becoming more and more ferocious and we couldn't just stand still. I set about ensuring that E and C had a long-term future.

BRIAN: Which is precisely *why* the Board appointed Bryony. She had a track record of shaking up complacency and moving organisations towards a viable future. One of my lads is a Down Syndrome kid so believe me my heart's right in this fight. I don't want to see too much of the charity dollar going to air sea rescue and surf lifesaving jet skis and rural ambulances and all that stuff, worthy as it is. The disadvantaged and disabled child is doing it tough out there and so are their parents and I want to see that message getting out there. And I think Bryony *is* getting that message out there and I'm deeply disappointed that her efforts have been met with what seems to me to be insidious internal opposition.

He looks directly at AMANDA *and* STELLA.

STELLA: Bryony told us she wanted to build on what we'd already achieved, but what we saw was more like a total dismantlement of everything we'd given years of our lives to build up. What was so wrong with the way we were doing things, Brian? Our income was going up steadily year by year.

BRYONY: Yes, but for how much longer?

STELLA: Our last three years before you came were the biggest income increases ever.

BRYONY: We were barely keeping pace with inflation.

STELLA: Three or four percent above inflation.

BRIAN: The Board wanted better than three or four percent. Across the sector donations have been increasing by fourteen to seventeen percent.

STELLA: You're not getting anywhere near that now.

BRYONY: I keep saying this to you, Stella, but you don't appear to be listening. The strategy I've put into place is long-term. I know last year was a tad disappointing, but this year is looking much better, right Cassie?

CASSIE: As far as we can tell. Yes.

BRYONY: Can we just get one thing clear? Like Brian, I have a personal stake in this. My cousin is a Cerebral Palsy victim. I know how something like that impacts on a family. I want to win the fight for the charity dollar. And even if this year's figures don't turn out to be quite what we hoped either, in five years or so my strategy will be paying off in a big way.

GIULIA: It certainly will.

BRIAN: When *can* we get this year's figures, Cassie? The Board was expecting them some time back.

GIULIA: There're a few tiny glitches in the new software, Brian. A week or two.

    BRIAN *frowns but restrains himself.*

JACK: What was it that specifically worried you about Bryony's new directions, Stella?

STELLA: Our success has always been based on soliciting donations through the mail. A simple but effective appeal sent to a carefully targeted database which I make sure is up to date. Now I know we've got to go into new areas such as direct donations off the Internet, and email reminders, I'm all for that, but to plan to phase out mail appeals because they're said to be 'stone age' just seemed very risky.

BRYONY: 'Stone age' are your words, Stella. I never used them.

STELLA: I beg to disagree, but let's not get bogged down on who said what. I did think and I still think that the new strategy was too risky.

BRYONY: Junk mail isn't even opened these days.

STELLA: Ours was.

BRYONY: For how much longer? The charities that are showing the greatest income growth curves all round the world are those that have switched to TV advertising and direct phone appeal.
STELLA: Some have. Others have failed.
BRYONY: The well-managed ones have succeeded.
JACK: Amanda, it seems that Stella had reservations about the new strategy? How did you feel?
AMANDA: I had doubts.
JACK: Did you say anything?
AMANDA: Not at first. But when Stella came under pressure I felt duty bound to support her.
JACK: And?
AMANDA: Well, up to that point I felt that Bryony and I were getting on well.
BRYONY: We were.
AMANDA: A couple of days before I'd even taken her round a casserole when she was shifting apartments.
BRYONY: Which I really appreciated.
AMANDA: And even when I did express some reservations, Bryony seemed to take it very well. Giulia seemed much more irritated than Bryony. It wasn't until later that I found out Bryony had been very critical of me to the Board.
BRYONY: I expressed disappointment. You didn't seem to be thinking things through. Just supporting Stella out of loyalty.
JACK: [*to* STELLA] Could you be more specific about the reservations you had about Bryony's new strategy?
STELLA: TV advertising is very, very high-cost. And so is hiring a battery of cold phone callers to follow up. And as Financial Controller I wanted to be sure that increased revenue was going to more than cover it.
BRYONY: Nobody can give you that sort of guarantee until it's tried.
STELLA: The first year's figures showed my fears were justified. Our net income actually *decreased* by three percent. Which put a strain on all our programs.
BRYONY: I told the Board there might be a short-term decrease in revenue. This is a long-term plan.
BRIAN: The Board weren't worried at all over that first year result. We gave Bryony our total backing.

STELLA: We're still waiting to see this year's results. And I for one will be very interested.
JACK: That was all that was worrying you, Stella. The financial aspect?
STELLA: Frankly, no it wasn't. It was also the nature of the TV ads themselves. Particularly this year's. The first series of TV ads were at least relatively restrained and tasteful—
GIULIA: They just didn't happen to work.
STELLA: But this year's ads featuring a disabled child appealing directly for funds seemed—
JACK: What?
STELLA: Tacky.
BRYONY: Tacky? You think little Sharon is tacky?
STELLA: No, Sharon is delightful. Exploiting her disability seemed tacky. And the process we used to find Sharon was even more tacky.
AMANDA: It was like we were running a talent quest for the cutest Down Syndrome kid in the country.
BRYONY: What did you want me to do? Spend all the advertising budget on a kid that had no appeal?
GIULIA: The dollars we collect ease the lives of thousands like Sharon.
STELLA: Pity about little Katrina.
BRIAN: We all know the Katrina incident was a setback.
BRYONY: I wouldn't even call it a setback, Brian. It was a momentary media flutter, now all but forgotten.
BRIAN: I hope you're right. The Board is very concerned.
BRYONY: The public have all but forgotten it.
STELLA: You wish.
GIULIA: It was just a minor blip.
BRIAN: I'd call it more than that, Giulia.
BRYONY: Katrina didn't try and kill herself.
AMANDA: Yes she did.
BRYONY: That was all media hype.
AMANDA: No it wasn't. She was devastated.
STELLA: And why wouldn't you be if you're a Down Syndrome kid who feels not much good for anything, then you're told you'd been selected to go in front of the cameras, then at the last minute you're dumped.
BRYONY: It was a hard call and I had to make it. Go and look at the two tapes Stella. Sharon, then Katrina, Then try and tell me I wasn't right.
AMANDA: Sharon might be 'cuter', but that isn't the point.

BRYONY: I'm afraid it very much *is* the point. If we're spending hundreds of thousands of dollars on a TV campaign, then we must have the right talent in front of camera. Good God, people have disappointments every day and they don't try to kill themselves.

AMANDA: [*upset*] We're talking about a severely disabled child. When she saw the words she was supposed to say being said by Sharon, she was devastated. I was the one who spoke to her parents.

BRYONY: Why in the hell did her parents let her see it?

AMANDA: They didn't mean to. And that made them doubly upset.

STELLA: If we'd done what Amanda had suggested, the parents wouldn't have gone to the media about it.

BRIAN: What was suggested?

AMANDA: I told Giulia that we should send the whole family off on holiday for a week or two at Hayman Island or somewhere. They indicated that they'd really appreciate it and I sensed that would have been the end of the matter. Giulia initially said it was a great idea.

BRIAN: It would have been. Why wasn't it done?

GIULIA: I got worried about the expense.

BRIAN: Why didn't you take the scheme to Bryony? I'm sure she would've seen its potential.

GIULIA: [*looking at* BRYONY] I should have. I'm sorry.

BRIAN: If Bryony had had any worries she could have brought it straight to the Board and we would have authorised it immediately.

GIULIA: I'm really sorry.

BRIAN: Let's hope that avalanche of bad publicity didn't hurt us, but I'd be personally surprised if it didn't. When you get headlines like 'The Caring Body that doesn't give a damn', that goes straight into the public consciousness and stays there a long time.

GIULIA: I'm really sorry.

BRIAN: I have to say, Giulia, that's a very big error of judgement.

BRYONY: Yes it was and I was disappointed that it wasn't brought to me, but the damage is done. However I'm certain the long-term impact will be negligible.

BRIAN: We shouldn't still be guessing. We should have had the figures by now.

BRYONY: Cassie is working on them day and night.

BRIAN: Exactly when *are* we going to get those figures, Cassie?

CASSIE: This new software is causing problems everywhere it's been installed.
BRIAN: Call in the suppliers.
BRYONY: We have. The problem is almost fixed. Look, whatever the figures show, the real damage to our income would have happened if we'd have gone to air with the wrong girl. It was a tough, tough call, but I had to take the long view. That's what I thought I'd been given the job to do, Brian. Make the tough calls.
BRIAN: I just wish that the holiday option had been considered.
BRYONY: Katrina *was* a setback and I accept ultimate responsibility, but I'm absolutely sure television appeals and random phoning are the way to go. Next year's child is sensational. One of our people alerted us to this little seven-year-old called Jill.
BRIAN: You'd be pushing to find a Down Syndrome child more personable than Sharon.
GIULIA: Jill's *not* actually Down Syndrome, Brian.
BRIAN: Cerebral Palsy?
BRYONY: Giulia's market research is telling her there's a bit of a compassion burn-out on the mentally impaired. Right, Giulia?
GIULIA: Right. Socially disadvantaged kids seem to be the way to go these days. The empathy pull of a neglected child with druggie parents like little Jill is huge.
BRYONY: I've got her photo in here somewhere.

    BRYONY *fishes in her handbag.*

GIULIA: She's just adorable. I've sort of half adopted her.
BRYONY: We both have. Her parents are in jail. Here it is.

    She hands a photo from her handbag to BRIAN.

BRIAN: Looks appealing.
BRYONY: She's brilliant.

    BRIAN *hands the photo back and* BRYONY *places it in front of her.*

JACK: So Amanda. When you first voiced doubts, you thought Bryony had taken your criticisms on board. What about you, Stella? Is that what you thought?
STELLA: No. I'm not as trusting as Amanda. I felt Bryony's perpetual smile was a cover-up.
JACK: Covering what?

STELLA: Anger. And, boy, was I right. She was bad mouthing us to the Board in a big way as soon as we first questioned her.

BRYONY: That's simply not true. Brian, you were there. Was I 'bad mouthing' them?

BRIAN: You voiced concern that your principal lieutenants didn't seem to be sharing your vision.

BRYONY: Was my language intemperate or abusive?

BRIAN: You seemed very low-key about it as I recall.

STELLA: That's not what I heard.

BRYONY: Who exactly is your source?

STELLA: Another Board member.

BRIAN: Are you telling me you went and quizzed a Board member?

STELLA: They came to me.

JACK: Why?

STELLA: They'd known me for years. They had confidence in my judgement and abilities and frankly they were appalled at the sort of things that were being said about Mandy and I.

BRIAN: Bryony made some strong but calm and considered comments about perceived obstruction, but in my opinion they were things the Board needed to know.

STELLA: They were strong all right. Enough to shock at least one Board member.

BRIAN: Yes and I think I know who your informant is, but let me just say again that we appointed Bryony to spearhead change. At least *some* of us on the Board felt the working atmosphere had become a tad too cosy under Alan Twomey's leadership, lovely man that he undoubtedly was. A good leader shouldn't be loved. They should be respected. And yes, when necessary, feared.

JACK: What did your informant claim was said, Stella?

BRYONY: This is second-hand hearsay.

JACK: [*indicating* BRIAN] We have a first-hand witness to dispute it.

STELLA: That Mandy and I didn't have the skills to cope with a new charity era, that we'd had it too easy for too long, and were basically dead weights.

BRYONY: Brian, was that what was said?

BRIAN: Not in language like that. You *did* express fears that I felt were legitimate.

JACK: [*to* STELLA] How did you react?

STELLA: How do you think? Not positively. But just as worrying was the fact that Amanda and I realised we were dealing with a boss who said one thing to your face and something very different behind your back.

BRYONY: There is absolutely nothing sinister about all this. I considered Stella and Amanda's criticisms, came to the conclusion that they were misplaced, and said so in calm terms to the Board.

STELLA: Why didn't you ever repeat these criticisms to my face?

BRYONY: I might have if I hadn't heard that you were referring to me as a two-headed snake.

STELLA: I said it once. And I know which one of your spy network took it back to you.

BRYONY: There was no 'spy' network.

STELLA: You recruited your inner sanctum very carefully.

CASSIE: There was no 'spying'. I happen to admire Bryony and her leadership and when you were so vicious about her it really upset me.

STELLA: So you went and told her everything?

CASSIE: I let her know when she was being white-anted behind her back. It's called loyalty.

STELLA: While all the time pretending to agree with everything we said.

CASSIE: That's not true.

STELLA: Did you ever *once* say, 'Hey, I don't agree with what you're saying. In my opinion Bryony is the most brilliant human being I have ever set eyes on'? Not likely.

CASSIE: I was your assistant. I wasn't about to cut my own throat.

STELLA: You got your loyalty reward in the end, didn't you? My job.

BRYONY: She got the promotion she deserved.

STELLA: In case you haven't noticed, Bryony, she's not coping well at all.

CASSIE: I'm fine.

STELLA: If you want the software problems Cassie's struggling with ironed out, then get me out of the useless job you've shunted me into, and put me back in charge of finance.

BRYONY: Forward Strategy a useless job?

STELLA: You dictate forward strategy, Bryony. I just research the viability of your plans. Why don't you tell Brian the truth? I was kicked sideways hoping I'd be so embarrassed I'd resign.

CASSIE: I'll have the figures in just a few weeks.

STELLA: In case you've forgotten, Brian, I used to get you figures on time. The Board's presently in the extraordinary position of not having a clue how we're travelling this year. Aren't you a little worried?

CASSIE: The new system will be infinitely better than the old one.

STELLA: Once you get it working.

BRYONY: The problem will be solved shortly. Can we move on?

JACK: Back to chronology. After Stella found out that Bryony had been critical of she and Amanda, things obviously started deteriorating fast. How do you see what happened next from your point of view, Bryony?

BRYONY: Resistance to anything that I suggested or Giulia suggested intensified. The initial TV launch was approaching and Stella was still digging her heels in and insisting we should do an exhaustive survey of all the US organisations that had gone down the same path.

STELLA: I simply did what any Financial Controller with any competence would do.

CASSIE: It was just a tactic to delay things.

STELLA: It was prudence.

JACK: You were the Assistant Financial Controller at that time, Cassie?

CASSIE: Right.

JACK: And you didn't have any qualms.

CASSIE: Every situation is unique. What happens in other organisations can't really tell us much about what would happen here. And in any case it was Bryony's call. I felt we should be backing her judgement.

BRYONY: I went to the Board and got permission to go ahead with or without Stella's approval.

BRIAN: We felt we had to back our CEO's judgement. That's what we put her there for.

JACK: So a study was never done?

STELLA: Oh yes. I still did it and it showed that sometimes the tactic worked and in many other cases it had driven the organisation to the wall. I gave it to Bryony but to my knowledge she still hasn't looked at it.

CASSIE: Because the data's not relevant.

BRYONY: I did read it and it said what I already knew. The well-managed organisations did very well out if it. The rest didn't. I was confident I could make it work and despite last year's minor financial set back and this year's media beat-up, I'm still convinced that long-term we have absolutely made the right decision.

JACK: So the new campaign was launched and the phone callers started. What happened then?

BRYONY: Well, of course there was a new target, wasn't there? Suddenly the Financial Controller had my entertainment budget under extraordinarily close scrutiny.

STELLA: I found the sums Bryony was spending on corporate entertainment hard to justify.

BRYONY: The expenditure was totally in line with contemporary practice.

STELLA: Maybe if we were a organisation that had to try and flog off a shonky product it might be justified, but to be honest, and Bryony sue me if you want to—you're always threatening to—the amount of money you're dragging out of E and C to wine and dine corporate bosses and take them to the opera and ballet or whatever is unconscionable. So much so in my opinion that someone might be excused for thinking your first priority isn't disadvantaged kids, but getting yourself splashed across the media on opening nights. And ingratiating yourself with all the big names in the city.

BRIAN: Stella, that really is actionable.

BRYONY: No, no. I hoped this would come out. Let her hang herself with her own rope. We're seeing the real agenda here. Resentment, envy and bile.

BRIAN: It is a very disappointing attitude you're taking, Stella. Corporate donations are a vital part of our income stream.

STELLA: We were doing just as well in that area before Bryony came here and started the great credit card blow-out.

BRYONY: Corporate sponsorship has gone up markedly.

STELLA: Deduct expenses and I bet we're almost exactly where we were.

CASSIE: You two just don't understand the meaning of the word long-term. This strategy is going to pay off big-time if you'd give it a chance.

BRYONY: They never will. If only you'd realise it, Stella, high-level corporate entertaining is very hard work. Try it some time. Remembering names, designations, shaping the flow of conversation—frankly I often come home to Ken and say, 'No more'. It can be utterly, utterly exhausting.

STELLA: Save yourself from all that exhaustion, Bryony. Alan and Amanda had just as much success going along and chatting to corporate heads in their offices.

BRYONY: If you think a low-key folksy approach is going to keep working in this era, then you're deluding yourself.

BRIAN: Dear old Alan was charming in his eccentric way, but honestly, thank God he's gone.

AMANDA: [*passionately*] Alan was one of the most loved people I've ever known. Okay, he'd stumble during every speech he ever made and get his facts wrong and he was terrible at remembering names—

BRIAN: You're not kidding. I got Barry, Bruce, Roger, Ralph, Richard—

AMANDA: [*intensely*] They knew he cared. About the children. They knew he *cared*.

BRYONY: And I don't? Then tell me why it is that I've got little Jill at my apartment just about every weekend?

STELLA: So you can claim that you're very close when you star with her on our next series of TV ads.

There's a silence. BRYONY*'s eyes narrow as she turns to* GIULIA.

GIULIA: I haven't told anyone.

STELLA: You don't think she'd tell us anything, Bryony. The ad agency brief came through the fax machine when I was sending something.

BRIAN: You're going on camera, Bryony?

BRYONY: It's a thought, Brian. I didn't suggest it, the ad agency did. When they saw little Jill and I together they thought we had such a good rapport that it would great if we just chatted. Jill would tell me what E and C had meant to her life. It's just a thought at this stage.

There's another silence.

JACK: Again, tracking back in sequence, the next point of major friction seems to have been the gala ball. Could you tell us about this, Bryony?

BRYONY: Giulia and I decided that the very best way to launch little Sharon as the new public face of disability was a gala charity ball. I delegated Amanda to organise it and if I hadn't stepped in at the last moment it would have been a total disaster.

AMANDA: You didn't give me enough time.
BRYONY: The time frame was tight, but certainly not impossible.
AMANDA: It was totally impossible.
BRYONY: It was a case of go then, when the social calendar wasn't so crowded, or wait another six months when it would've been far too late.
AMANDA: I did the very best I could.
BRYONY: You booked a venue twice as large as we needed.
AMANDA: Based on the figures you gave me.
BRYONY: They were initial estimates. The ballroom was half empty and the media turn-up was pathetic.
AMANDA: The media was Giulia's responsibility.
GIULIA: [*hurt*] I wouldn't call the press turn-out 'pathetic', Bryony. We had an okay turn-up. I thought you were reasonably happy.
BRYONY: I'm not pointing the finger, Giulia. It all could have been so much better.
AMANDA: Most of the media who did turn up were the ones I contacted.
GIULIA: That's not true.
STELLA: Yes it is.
AMANDA: Considering the time we had and the logistical nightmares, it was a wonder it went as well as it did.
BRIAN: I think you're being a bit too harsh on yourself, Bryony. I thought it was quite a good night.
BRYONY: The hall was half empty.
AMANDA: I was on the phone for eighteen hours straight for three days to get the numbers we did get.
BRIAN: The hall certainly didn't look half empty to me.
BRYONY: That was only because of my creative use of space.
GIULIA: And we did raise two hundred thousand and little Sharon was in two of the papers next day.
BRYONY: Buried on page twenty. But look, I accept my share of the blame and I did to the Board.
STELLA: That's not what I heard.
BRYONY: Whoever your Deep Throat was, they're wrong. I accepted my share of the blame and Brian can confirm that.
BRIAN: You certainly weren't happy with the way things went, but I can't remember exactly what was said.

AMANDA: Let me remind you, Brian. She called me a 'whiner' who 'dropped her bundle' at the first hint of pressure and told the Board she'd like to get rid of me.

BRIAN: She said she was going to reprimand you, and that you might have to be let go.

AMANDA: Luckily most of the Board had been to the ball and thought it wasn't nearly the disaster Bryony painted it as, and the majority of the Board didn't want to fire me. Despite the fact that you urged them to, Brian.

BRIAN: It was nothing personal. I just think that when the CEO feels they can't work with someone anymore they have to be backed.

AMANDA: Most of the Board have known me for many years, Brian, and they know I'm not the type of person Bryony was painting me as.

BRIAN: Amanda, I don't doubt you've done great service over the years, but new directions need new types of skills.

JACK: You did want Amanda fired, Bryony?

BRYONY: Yes I did. And I still do.

From left: Trudy Hellier as Tamsyn, Tammy McCarthy as Cassie, Michael Fry as Jack, Carole Patullo as Amanda, Margaret Mills as Stella, Denis Moore as Brian and Vivienne Walshe as Bryony in the 2001 La Mama production in Melbourne. (Photo: David van Royen)

JACK: So how did you feel when the Board refused to do it?
BRYONY: Betrayed. I'd been brought in to lead and then told I couldn't. But I'm mature enough to realise that decisions don't always go your way and I just got on with the job as best I could.
STELLA: [*grunting with disgust*] Sure.
JACK: Stella?
STELLA: When she couldn't fire Mandy, plan two was to make her life so hellish she'd be forced to resign.
BRYONY: That's libellous.
STELLA: Sue me then.
BRYONY: If you ever say it outside this room, I will.
STELLA: She's been trying to make my life hell too, but I've got a tougher hide than Mandy.
BRYONY: Stella, this is a total fantasy of yours. I certainly wasn't happy with either of you and said so directly and calmly, but there was certainly never any concerted campaign to get rid of you. Please credit me with a little bit of decency and professionalism.
TAMSYN: [*vehemently*] The truth is both of you are just plain paranoid. The truth is there's no clique or inner sanctum that's out to get you. The truth is that Bryony is an inspiring leader and most around the place admire her and want to help realise her vision.
BRYONY: Thank you, Tamsyn.
TAMSYN: I've had to sit here listening to all this paranoid nonsense and frankly it's making me sick.
CASSIE: It's just a case of the old guard digging in its heels and I'm sick of it too.
TAMSYN: I've had to listen to their bile for far too long. The Board should do what a board is supposed to do. Back Bryony and get rid of the two of them.
STELLA: Any comments we made about Bryony you seemed only too happy to hear. How come you didn't tell us to stop the 'bile' either?
TAMSYN: My job is to listen to complaints impartially. Which I tried to do, but in the end it just wore me down. And for your information none of it went back to Bryony.
BRYONY: Don't worry. I heard it all from other sources. The two of them apparently took enormous exception to the fact I drive a European convertible, that I live in a comfortable high-rise apartment with a view, that my partner Ken is well-off, that I wear clothes with

a designer label, and that I take the trouble to exercise and watch my diet. I know all the names. As well as the Two-Headed Snake, I get Bryony the Bitch, Aerobic Annie, Mercedes Lady, and they call Ken 'Lockjaw'.

JACK: 'Lockjaw'?

BRYONY: I'm not sure why.

STELLA: On social occasions he never gets to open his mouth. Too embarrassed to tell her that, Cassie?

CASSIE: Why shouldn't I tell her what you say? When you two were being so vicious, why shouldn't I tell her?

STELLA: We didn't use any of those names until she started targeting us. You think *we* were vicious? We were just babes in the woods.

BRYONY: I did not target anyone. And if you say it again I *will* consider legal action.

JACK: Threatening legal action isn't helpful, Bryony. We're here today to be as open as possible. Amanda, did you feel you were targeted?

BRYONY: I don't want this avenue pursued. Is that clear?

JACK: Bryony, we're all here as equals today. If you start trying to dictate the agenda, I'll have to call this off.

> BRYONY *is about to say something when* BRIAN *touches her arm in a signal to let it be.*

Amanda, did you feel you were being targeted?

BRYONY: It's a fantasy they've dreamed up.

TAMSYN: Absolutely.

AMANDA: Yes I did. After the charity ball Bryony called me into her office and closed the door, then she turned around and just stared at me for what seemed like minutes with a look of total hatred on her face, and then let fly with this unbelievable tirade of abuse.

BRYONY: That's another fantasy. In fact I did what managers are supposed to do. I gave Amanda direct and honest feedback about her recent performance.

STELLA: Yeah, sure.

BRYONY: I don't seem to recall you being there, Stella.

AMANDA: If that was just direct and honest feedback, I'd hate to ever be abused.

BRYONY: I was tough. I admit I was tough. Maybe a tad too tough, but I felt it was warranted. You two had been pushing me to the absolute

limit. [*To* JACK] It had got past passive resistance, the two of them were actively trying to sabotage the new policy directions I'd put in place.
STELLA: I questioned their wisdom. I still do. When this year's income figures finally emerge I'll be very interested.
JACK: Can you remember what you *did* say behind that closed door, Bryony?
BRYONY: Almost to the word. I told her that I was disappointed that she'd chosen to oppose the direction I'd taken, and that I suspected that her poor performance in the organisation of the ball was deliberate, and that it might be wise if she considered alternative employment.
TAMSYN: Which as the head of Human Resources I feel was totally appropriate, and would have in fact advised if I'd been asked.
JACK: Is that your memory of what was said, Amanda?
AMANDA: No it isn't.
BRYONY: I'm sure it wouldn't be.
JACK: [*to* AMANDA] What *was* your memory of what was said?
AMANDA: I'm not sure I really want to talk about it. It still makes me incredibly upset. No one has ever looked at me or spoken to me in that way in my life.
BRYONY: Then your life's been very, very sheltered.
JACK: Could you tell us?
TAMSYN: Jack, I'm a professional in this field and this sort of situation— 'You said this', 'No I didn't', ad infinitum, gets us absolutely nowhere.
JACK: Let's see. Amanda, could you tell us your version. You said no one had looked at you like that before.
AMANDA: Hatred. Fury. It was genuinely frightening.
BRYONY: Tamsyn's right. It's one person's word against another and we should stop this right now.
JACK: Bryony. You seem determined to take control of this meeting. It's not how it works.
BRYONY: Brian, could we call this off? It's a useless exercise that seems designed to demean me.
BRIAN: The Board has asked that we do this, Bryony. I know how you're feeling, but if you could bear with it, I'd appreciate it.
BRYONY: When we're about to get what's obviously going to be a highly-coloured version of events, what's the point?

BRIAN: Bryony, I don't believe everything I hear. I know how professional you are and I'm not inclined to believe you'd ever behave anything other than professionally.

BRYONY: I can imagine what she's going to say, and I don't want to have to sit here and listen to her lie.

AMANDA: I don't lie.

BRYONY: You'd better not. I'm warning you.

JACK: Bryony.

AMANDA: It was very harsh, very personal and I'm still quite devastated by it. I'd rather not go into details.

JACK: I think you should.

BRYONY: You're on her side. It's blatantly obvious.

JACK: I'm on nobody's side. We need to hear Amanda's version so we can understand how she's feeling. Amanda?

AMANDA: [*trying to control tears*] She said I was just a pathetic fat blob and that everyone despised me, that I was one of the world's great losers, and that looking at me and the way I dressed made her want to vomit. And that was just the start.

BRYONY: That's it. I'm not listening to any more of these lies.

She gets up to go.

JACK: That's up to you. But it will effectively end this process.

BRYONY: Brian, can you see just how difficult this is for me?

BRIAN: It's difficult for all of us, Bryony, but I think the Board would prefer it if you stayed.

BRYONY *looks at him, suddenly aware that her behaviour is threatening to lose her his support.*

BRYONY: If you'd rather me stay, I'll stay.

BRIAN: I really appreciate it.

JACK: Amanda?

AMANDA: [*tears still in her eyes*] She went on to say that I was a total embarrassment around the place, and a disaster as one of the public faces of E and C. She said she felt like hiding me in a cupboard on social occasions and that I was seething with hatred for her because she was slim and attractive and socially poised and articulate. She said she'd had that kind of petty hatred right up to here, and that if I wanted a fight then I'd well and truly got one because she didn't

intend to let a fat pathetic frump with no more dress sense than a bag lady make her life a total misery.
BRYONY: Brian, can you honestly imagine me ever speaking like that?
BRIAN: Whatever was said, it's obvious that the working relationship between the two of you has become untenable.
BRYONY: You *can* believe I said something like that?
BRIAN: No I can't, but whatever was said, the relationship's become untenable.
BRYONY: Something I've been telling the Board for some time.
BRIAN: When I report back to the Board about today, I'm sure they'll realise the situation can't go on.
BRYONY: I hope so.
JACK: Amanda, how did you react?
AMANDA: To what Bryony said? I didn't. I was in a total state of shock. I've always prided myself that I get on pretty well with people and I've never been spoken to like that in my life, so I was in total shock. I mean I'm not naïve. I knew I wasn't Bryony's favourite person on planet earth, but as far as I was concerned I'd been voicing legitimate worries and been doing the best I could at the tasks I'd been assigned. But suddenly I knew the real situation. Just how hated and despised I was. I was so shocked in fact that I didn't even realise I was crying until I heard Bryony say, 'For God's sake, don't do the teary-eyed thing'. She told me that instead of standing there feeling sorry for myself I should have the discipline to go on a crash diet and get out of E and C and get myself a life. As I…

AMANDA, *tears in her eyes, can't go on. There's a brief silence.*

BRYONY: All I can say, Amanda, is that you've got a very vivid imagination.
AMANDA: As I stumbled to the door she said, 'And that's just the start. Get used to the idea that if you stay around here your life will be living hell. Believe me.' And I believed her.
BRYONY: Haven't you forgotten a few details? That I twirled my cape, breathed fire and hurled my pitchfork at you?
STELLA: I talked to her right after she came out of there. I believe every word she just said.
BRYONY: I have never even remotely used language like that to anyone in my life.

JACK: What did you do then, Amanda?

AMANDA: I wanted to resign. I couldn't bear the thought of any more of that. But Stella said that that was just what Bryony wanted. She said I should stay and fight. But I wasn't sure that I could. I was still shaking for hours afterwards. It wasn't just the anger that shook me, it was the contempt.

BRYONY: I spoke directly and honestly and didn't mince words. But I never resort to personal abuse.

AMANDA: I felt that Bryony had no more respect for me than she would for a... worm. It was a feeling I didn't ever want to have again. I'm human. I need to feel liked and respected. But suddenly I felt as if I'd entered totally new territory. I just wanted to run.

BRYONY: I'm sorry, Amanda, but this is just a totally hysterical reaction to a routine dressing down.

AMANDA: [*suddenly angry*] Ridicule me, Bryony. Mock me with that bloody awful smile of yours, but you know damn well it's true. Every word of it.

There's an electric silence. BRYONY *defiantly retains eye contact with* AMANDA, *but finally looks away.*

BRYONY: Suppose I did say a few things that were ill-considered, and for the life of me I can't remember doing it. But suppose I did. Most people wouldn't treat that like the end of the world was nigh. They'd say, 'Gee, Bryony is really, really upset. She must be at the end of her tether. Maybe I have been pushing her too hard. Maybe I have overstepped the mark. Maybe it isn't fun for her to have come here with a mission to change E and C's culture to one that will survive far into the future and find herself criticised and undermined every step of the way. Maybe she resents the fact that despite the fact she works seventy or eighty hours a week for this place all she gets is abuse and mule-like resistance. Maybe I should start trying to see things from her viewpoint.' We're all human, Amanda, and at that point I felt stressed to breaking point, but instead of taking that on board you decide that I've organised some nefarious plot to victimise you on a long-term basis. And you proceed to turn this paranoid fantasy into a self-fulfilling prophecy by your continued truculence and bingo, we're all aboard the disaster express.

JACK: You think maybe you did use some personal language, Bryony?

BRYONY: Maybe I did. For the life of me I honestly can't remember. The point I was trying to make was that people do this when they're extremely stressed. And other people realise that. And don't collapse in a weeping heap. The world is a tough place. No one was ever sweet to me when I was surviving and making the best of some of the worst schools in this country. I'd like a dollar for every time someone's said personal things to me. For God's sake, what kind of sheltered life have you led, Amanda?

AMANDA: A life where no one's treated me like you have.

JACK: You didn't resign, Amanda. Why?

AMANDA: I started to get angry. Very angry. I couldn't sleep at night. I used to go over and over that scene in the office in my mind trying to work out whether any of her accusations were true. Or partly true. 'Fat pathetic frump'. Was I? 'No more dress sense than a bag lady'. True? 'Seething with resentment'? Was I? Fat? I could hardly deny that one.

BRYONY: The word was never mentioned.

AMANDA: Fat. Yes. It's a metabolism problem by the way, Bryony. No amount of dieting in the world will do me much good. I should know. I've tortured myself with them for about twenty years now. Frump? Yes, I've never been hugely attractive to men and it's something that's hurt and depressed me. It's awful to see eyes glide right over you on the way to someone more... exciting. School dances were absolute torture for me and it hasn't got any better since. Mind you, men have always *liked* me. Liked. She's cheerful and easy to get on with was the general verdict. Pleasant 'personality'. But almost none of them wanted to pursue it further than that. And the ones that did wanted little more than a sure-fire 'lay' because they knew I couldn't afford to be choosy. So 'frump'? Yes. But 'pathetic'? No. Not pathetic. That's where I dug my heels in. My assessments up to now have always said 'competent, cheerful, team player, good to be around, conscientious, wish there were more like her around here'. That's not pathetic. Well, to be honest, they did also say 'could be more assertive'. Which is a bit pathetic. I shouldn't have gone into deep shock when Bryony screamed at me. I should have screamed back, so I guess I am a little pathetic, but only a little. I kept playing and replaying that office scene in my head obsessively trying to work out what I should have said and when I should have said it. And I got angry with myself that I didn't. But if there was something pathetic about me I decided that there wouldn't be anymore. I decided that Stella was right. I shouldn't resign. I mustn't resign. I must stay and fight. And the truth was, when I reflected soberly, I didn't have all that many options. At my age and without a decent reference and with jobs in the charity sector very thin on the ground and having saved not nearly enough to even *begin* to think of retiring, I really was going to try and hang in there in any case. But I was going to need a little support. Stella said that the type of abuse I'd been subjected to was absolutely beyond the pale and I should go straight to Human Resources and be honest about what had happened to me. Human Resources, said Stella, is there to help overcome difficulties and frictions. So off I went to Tamsyn to report the threats and ask her advice about what to do.

STELLA: Big mistake.

From left: Margaret Mills as Stella, Denis Moore as Brian and Vivienne Walshe as Bryony on the 2001 La Mama production in Melbourne. (Photo: David van Royen)

AMANDA: Tamsyn had always seemed warm and friendly in the past. In fact she'd been the one who'd convinced me I had the ability to take on some marketing and PR work while Alan was still the boss. She'd even sent me on some short courses to increase my skills.

JACK: So you went to see Tamsyn?

AMANDA: [*nodding*] And Tamsyn seemed quite sympathetic and told me that it was obvious I'd been through a rough spell and that she'd talk to Bryony.

JACK: Is that how you remember the conversation, Tamsyn?

TAMSYN: More or less, although Amanda is reading in more than there was when she says I was sympathetic.

JACK: You weren't sympathetic?

TAMSYN: I was professionally neutral. I listened to Amanda's version and then checked it against Bryony's.

JACK: And when you did?

TAMSYN: I thought Bryony was very up-front and honest. She admitted she'd been a little harsher than possibly she should have been, and was a little worried on that account.

BRYONY: I still totally deny saying anything personal.

TAMSYN: But look, it's my job to monitor workplace friction and I'd started to despair about how bad the vibes were getting. It reflects on me as a professional when things get this bad. I told Bryony that in all honesty she'd been very controlled for a long time and a blow-up was long overdue.

STELLA: You knew which side your bread was buttered on.

TAMSYN: I've already made no secret of the fact that I admire the new spirit Bryony has brought to the place and it's saddened and angered me to see her hobbled by the kind of resentment and malice she's talked about today. There was no doubt in my mind that Amanda *believed* she'd endured something out of the ordinary, but I also think that Bryony's right when she says that Amanda and Stella have lived in very sheltered circumstances for a long while and got used to doing things exactly as they liked.

STELLA: [*indicating* CASSIE, TAMSYN *and* GIULIA] These three know where the power lies. If leader attacks Amanda then Amanda is a dead duck, so the best career move is to fall in behind leader and help her finish the job.

TAMSYN: [*upset*] It was my professional judgement, Stella. You know I can't be bought and sold.

STELLA: I know you couldn't once. But it's a brave soul who takes the victim's side when a bully enters a schoolyard.

BRYONY: Now who's calling people names?

JACK: Using a word like 'bully' isn't going to help us, Stella.

BRYONY: Thank you. The first bit of recognition that I'm under constant attack.

STELLA: I'm tougher than Amanda, but I've gone through my own hell and I came here today to say what I think.

JACK: Maybe take a second or two to think before you say. Tamsyn, you're saying that you felt Bryony had just cause?

TAMSYN: I believed that Amanda deserved to be reprimanded and that she had overreacted due to a low tolerance for conflict and stress.

STELLA: [*to the three younger women*] You lot are real survivors, aren't you?

GIULIA: No. We're just younger, better trained, and more aware that the world is changing faster than at any time in human history.

CASSIE: We're the future. That's our only crime.

JACK: What happened then, Amanda?

AMANDA: I went home at the weekend fairly confident that Tamsyn, if not taking my side, would at least be sympathetic. Going to her had actually made me a lot calmer and less stressed. I thought maybe Bryony would feel as if she couldn't get away with that sort of behaviour anymore and I'd have some sort of protection. My mum noticed that my mood had picked up and said, 'Thank God for that'. Then on Sunday morning the phone rang and it was Bryony on the line. And if what she said in the office was bad, this was worse.

BRYONY: I won't deny that I was angry. You'd gone behind my back to Tamsyn and lied.

AMANDA: I don't lie!

BRYONY: I was angry. I won't deny it.

AMANDA: You screamed down the line.

BRYONY: I never ever raise my voice, let alone scream. I was angry but controlled.

JACK: [*to* AMANDA] What do you recall being said?

BRYONY: Brian, I know you're under pressure from the Board to complete this sordid and demeaning little witch-hunt, but I just can't sit here and listen to any more of this hysterical character assassination.
BRIAN: Bryony, I know it's painful, but if we leave things where they are now the situation will be worse than it ever was. We've started something and for everyone's sake I think we've got to see it through.
BRYONY: I hope when you report this back to the Board you'll frame it in such a way that they'll see the real perspective.
BRIAN: Bryony, I know how to read the truth of a situation.
BRYONY: It's just the bile of disgruntled employees.
BRIAN: That's undoubtedly a big factor.
BRYONY: I would have thought the *only* factor.
BRIAN: I have great faith in you, so don't ever think I'll lose sight of that.

BRYONY *is somewhat reassured. She nods.*

AMANDA: Brian, in plain language, are you saying you think I'm a liar?
BRIAN: The truth is often complex, and powerful emotions on both sides tend to make it difficult to arrive at.
BRYONY: I hope you aren't suggesting *I'm* a liar?
BRIAN: We've started down this track, could we just please finish it?
JACK: Amanda. The phone call?
AMANDA: Bryony tended to repeat the same points over and over, but in essence she said that my plan to whine to Tamsyn behind her back had well and truly backfired. She said that Tamsyn was absolutely disgusted at my attempt to demonise her, that Tamsyn totally believed her account of the meeting, that Tamsyn thought I was an hysterical neurotic with a borderline personality disorder, and that Tamsyn would be happy to put this all in a report which recommended to the Board that I be fired.
TAMSYN: That's not an accurate report of what I said.
AMANDA: Can I suggest the inaccuracy came from Bryony, not me.
BRYONY: No you cannot.
JACK: What's your recollection of what was said, Bryony?
BRYONY: I said in a calm voice—no screaming whatsoever—as I said I just don't scream. Ever—that any staff member had a perfect right to consult Tamsyn, but if allegations were made, they'd be answered.
JACK: You did say that Tamsyn had taken your side.
BRYONY: It was true.

JACK: Length of call?

BRYONY: Maximum ten minutes.

AMANDA: Over an hour. I took it on my mobile before I got on the train from my mother's place. The journey takes fifty-five minutes and I was still talking to Bryony after I got off.

BRYONY: I was very upset. I wasn't registering time.

AMANDA: Over an hour.

BRYONY: Whatever. The fact remains that a highly competent Human Resources executive had heard both sides of the story and come down heavily in my favour.

TAMSYN: I thought that any outburst, if it *had* happened, was in some degree, justified.

BRYONY: You expressed it more strongly than that. You said, 'About damn time someone let her have it'.

JACK: [*to* TAMSYN] But you didn't offer to recommend to the Board that Amanda be fired.

TAMSYN: No.

BRYONY: I didn't ever claim that she had.

JACK: And where did that leave you, Amanda?

AMANDA: Tamsyn said it was last chance time for me. I either had to make a big effort to adapt to the new corporate culture or clear my desk and get out. I said I had no intention of getting out.

JACK: What happened then?

AMANDA: The bad times started in earnest.

BRYONY: This is total paranoia. If there were any changes in Amanda's circumstances there were very good reasons which Tamsyn will explain.

TAMSYN: Certainly.

AMANDA: Whatever I say there'll of *course* be a perfectly good reason for it. Those two are very clever.

JACK: I still think we should hear your version.

AMANDA: They've covered their tracks perfectly. It'll just make me seem more and more paranoid.

STELLA: You did get a little bit paranoid, Mandy.

AMANDA: When Stella turned on me I knew I was in big trouble.

STELLA: I didn't *turn* on you. I just think you were a little bit too suspicious.

JACK: Tell us what happened, Amanda.

AMANDA: First of all I was shifted out of my office which is next to Stella's and sent down to a little hole under the stairs.
TAMSYN: We had to have Cassie nearer to Bryony. Financial control is central to everything.
AMANDA: I felt totally isolated.
CASSIE: You were put where I'd been and *I* hadn't complained.
AMANDA: Then I was called into Bryony's office and she told me that my job description was going to be revamped. About two or three days of the week I used to be out of the office visiting our various program centres. I knew all the directors and the staff and listened to their problems and made my own assessment of their progress and drew up recommendations for finance allocation. They all knew me and knew that my recommendations would be fair. There was scarcely ever any question raised about them. Suddenly I was told that there would be no more of that. I had to stay in my office and they'd have to submit lengthy applications which I'd process. So now they're all spending countless hours filling in forms so that their 'key performance indicators' can be measured and they're angry because it's taking them away from their real work.
CASSIE: It's a change that had to come, Amanda. In fact it was long overdue. Our income comes from our donors and we've got to be accountable for the way it's spent. Even Stella will admit that.
STELLA: We had to move to closer monitoring eventually.
AMANDA: The end result is going to be pretty much the same as it was, in any case.
BRYONY: The fact that we got by with the hit or miss methods of the past was more good luck than good management.
AMANDA: It wasn't good luck. I knew what was going on, and I was good at what I did.
STELLA: The person after you mightn't have been as good though, Mandy.
AMANDA: [*to* JACK] They'll come up with a perfectly good explanation for everything. Even Stella went over to their side.
STELLA: Mandy, that's rubbish.
AMANDA: I'm just paranoid. Right. Well, whatever the reason I really felt totally isolated. I was suddenly cut off from contact with everyone in here and everyone out in the field.

BRYONY: Amanda, I didn't want to bring this up, but the truth is you were spending more and more time just gossiping to the people 'out in the field', and less and less time assessing.

AMANDA: Getting to know the people *was* 'assessing'.

CASSIE: I'm sorry, but none of us had real confidence in your reports anymore. We had to have better data.

BRYONY: Precisely.

AMANDA: I'm sorry, but I remain to be convinced that all this extra mountain of paperwork is going to make your decisions one jot better.

JACK: [*to* AMANDA] You mentioned monitoring of phone calls?

AMANDA: I was the only one in the office, to my knowledge, who had to account for every outside call I made.

TAMSYN: There was a reason for that.

AMANDA: I sometimes rang my mother. She's got advanced Parkinson's. It's very distressing.

TAMSYN: Sometimes?

AMANDA: All right. I rang her once a day.

TAMSYN: Sometimes for up to half an hour.

AMANDA: Occasionally. When she was really upset. I mean, can any of you imagine what it's like for a super active woman like my mother not being able to control her limbs anymore?

BRYONY: We're sympathetic Amanda, but we've all got personal difficulties and there has to be a balance.

JACK: Okay, let's leave that for a moment. Stella? Do you feel you're being singled out at all.

STELLA: No. Just made to work on a project Bryony knows damn well I hate.

JACK: Which is?

BRYONY: Which is totally confidential.

JACK: [*to* STELLA] Can you talk about it in broad terms?

STELLA: I'm researching Bryony's new brainchild. The new direction she wants E and C to head in.

BRYONY: We're not here to discuss that today.

BRIAN: We're already going in a new direction.

STELLA: This is the *new* new direction.

BRYONY: I'm mapping out a new strategy, Brian. It's very tentative at this stage. Too tentative to take to the Board just yet.

BRIAN: What kind of new direction?

AMANDA: Getting out of the key areas of need into areas that'll get her more social kudos.

BRYONY: [*to* AMANDA] You would see it that way. Brian, these are very tentative plans and I don't think they should be discussed today.

STELLA: They're not tentative. They're thoroughly well worked out and ready to go.

BRIAN: I'd like to hear them. And I'd like to know why the Board hasn't heard about them?

BRYONY: There is nothing at all definite at this stage.

GIULIA: There's no need to apologise, Bryony. I think it's very exciting.

BRIAN: I really *would* like to hear, Bryony.

BRYONY: For any country to survive in the future it's got to stress knowledge, innovation and excellence. And I feel that E and C could play its part.

BRIAN: In what way?

BRYONY: I think we define 'disadvantage' too narrowly. The real areas of disadvantage are the children of the working class and the unemployed and the drug addicted. Like little Jill, who we're using in our next TV ads. I envisage a significant proportion of our income should be devoted to large-scale scholarship programs which identify talented young kids from poor families at a very early age. Those who are talented scholastically, sports wise, and artistically, so we could allow them to find their true potential and have them contribute to our 'excellence'. Think how many great artists, actors, scientists and sportsmen are out there waiting to be discovered. I find it a very exciting concept.

BRIAN: What about the *really* disadvantaged? Those with mental and physical deficits?

BRYONY: Part of the reason I'm making centres like our sheltered workshops more accountable is that research shows that if they're well run they can actually make a profit.

BRIAN: They can make some income, but—

BRYONY: Frankly, and this is the reason why Amanda had to be replaced, they've had it far too easy. Successful charity entrepreneurs are starting to hire out groups of disadvantaged workers to factories, and it's been very, very successful. They can manage a surprising range of industrial work and the government subsidy they get and their generally willing and cheerful nature, makes them a godsend for many employers. The very word 'sheltered workshop' tells us precisely what's wrong with the handout mentality.

BRIAN: I'm having a bit of trouble getting my brain around this, Bryony.

BRYONY: Brian, we won't be opting out of our obligations to the traditional disadvantaged. Even in the long term. I'm thinking in terms of large-scale paraplegic sports scholarships. In the long term I can even envisage co-funding a Para-Olympian sports institute. Look, all this is early stages and I hadn't meant it to come out today.

BRIAN: I'm rather glad it has.

BRYONY: And nothing is set in stone. But I am very excited at the general concept.

BRIAN: I'm sorry, but I'm not quite as excited as you are, Bryony. And this is not just because my own boy is Down Syndrome, but I'm very dubious as to whether the genuinely mentally and physically handicapped can ever really become self-supporting.

BRYONY: If that proves unrealistic then of course we'll stay in the field.

BRIAN: How long exactly has Stella been working on this new strategy?

STELLA: Around three months.

BRIAN: In all fairness, Bryony, I think the Board should have known about this. Quite a while ago.

BRYONY: I wanted it to be researched as thoroughly as possible before I brought it to you. And it should have been ready by now, but again, Stella has patently been dragging her feet.

GIULIA: Not kidding.

STELLA: Frankly I hate the idea. And to be totally honest I've sent a draft proposal to my Board contact who's outraged, so you'll hear about it soon, Brian.

BRYONY: That's a total breach of ethics.

STELLA: Yes it is. Sorry. I just thought this was too important. If your bloody plan's adopted it means a further abandoning of anyone who isn't potentially brilliant, and leaving them to either be exploited or rot.

BRYONY: We're not all born equal, Stella. And those with real potential should get every chance.

BRIAN: Bryony, irrespective of the merits or otherwise of this new direction of yours, I find it troubling that something so fundamental and radical wasn't brought to the Board much earlier.

BRYONY: [*losing her cool just slightly for the first time*] Brian, there are times when a CEO thinks that they are thinking ahead of the Board, and this was one of them. I'm sure you've done it yourself occasionally.

BRIAN: I can't speak for the Board, Bryony, but I have the feeling that they'll want to retain their commitment to the mentally and physically disadvantaged, and I suspect they'll feel that very strongly. Very strongly.

BRYONY: [*calm again*] Brian, it's just an idea. If the Board feels that way then of course I'll respect it. Cassie and Giulia came to me with the idea and I thought it was an idea worth researching. It would have had to go to the Board for approval. I don't see what the fuss is about.

BRIAN: Could I respectfully suggest that Cassie and Giulia think a little harder before coming up with a policy direction like that?

> CASSIE *and* GIULIA *look at each other, then at* BRYONY.

GIULIA: Sorry.

BRIAN: Giulia, you're young and still learning, but didn't you suspect that if E and C lessened its core commitment to the intellectually and physically disabled that the press backlash might have been even worse than we got over Katrina?

GIULIA: Yes I should've. I'm sorry.

BRIAN: Can you imagine the headlines. 'Charity dumps handicapped and opts for glamour'.

BRYONY: I don't think that's quite fair, Brian.

BRIAN: That's what the newspapers would do. You should have been aware of that yourself, Bryony.

BRYONY: Yes I should've. I take full responsibility. It's just that when your young staff come to you full of enthusiasm, it's hard not to want to encourage it. But in this case perhaps my judgement should have been better.

BRIAN: I think perhaps it should.

> BRYONY *bites her lip and stays calm and nods.*

JACK: Amanda, you did mention other things that were disturbing you at work.

AMANDA: My annual leave application was turned down and scheduled for the middle of winter.

TAMSYN: I did the best I could for you, Amanda, but not everyone can go on leave in summer.

AMANDA: The most distressing thing of all was that when Bryony or her cheer squad *did* talk to me it was to sneer.

TAMSYN: Now this is *really* paranoid.

AMANDA: Little jibes all the time. Little so-called 'jokes'.

JACK: About what?

AMANDA: Usually my weight. Every day there'd be another 'fat' joke or comment.

GIULIA: When?

AMANDA: When? Try the time you read the article in the paper—very loudly—about the woman who was forced to buy two plane tickets because she couldn't fit into one seat.

CASSIE: It was funny. It wasn't directed at you.

AMANDA: Then I wonder why everyone kept laughing for about three minutes then glancing across at me.

TAMSYN: It wasn't personal.

AMANDA: Excuse me. It *was* personal. And every time there was an article about weight loss or diets—the same thing. Either read out aloud or left on my desk.

CASSIE: We actually thought you might be interested in doing something about the problem.

AMANDA: And the day Giulia read out that list of the ten worst dressed women in the world, and Cassie said, 'They should have looked harder'. Glancing at me with a smirk. Do you think I'm stupid? And the final blow was starting to see Stella laughing with them.

STELLA: Mandy, who's been supporting you today?

AMANDA: You're fighting your own war with Bryony, so it suits you to support me.

STELLA: Sorry, that really is paranoid.

AMANDA: Right. So everyone's agreed. I'm paranoid.

STELLA: Amanda, you did drop your bundle and start to get pathetic.

AMANDA: It got to a point I couldn't cope.

STELLA: Applying for a week's compassionate leave when your cat died? Did you really expect to be taken seriously when you started doing things like that?

AMANDA: Yes that was pathetic. Stupid. It turned me into the office madwoman—well and truly.

STELLA: And the quality of your work was going steadily down.

AMANDA: I was depressed, for God's sake. Some days I was just sitting at my desk with the tears pouring out. If it hadn't have been for the terror of the thought of living on unemployment benefits I would've given in much sooner. But after the debacle of the cat episode I knew I'd lost the fight. Then on the very day I'm drafting my resignation letter, with exquisite timing, I get a letter telling me to return for a follow-up breast screening.

JACK: It must have been a huge blow.

AMANDA: Strangely enough it turned me round again. I could have sunk deeper into self pity but for some odd reason I got angry again. I suddenly wanted to fight, both for my life and my job. I had private health cover but this was going to be long term and I needed the job to keep up payments.

STELLA: There was a huge change. Okay, Amanda's right. I did turn my back on her for a while and I'm really ashamed of that. I guess I was in survival mode too. But suddenly there she is, her eyes are ablaze, and she's fighting again. I didn't know why at first because she didn't tell anyone.

AMANDA: The operation was coming up and I finally had to. And there was going to be a long course of chemo after. I went to Tamsyn.

JACK: How did Tamsyn react?

AMANDA: Quite sympathetically.

TAMSYN: I'm not a monster.

JACK: When Tamsyn told you, Bryony, how did you react?

BRYONY: I was sympathetic too.

JACK: You went and spoke to Amanda?

BRYONY: I wrote her a note.

AMANDA: After I'd had the operation.

JACK: A note?

BRYONY: It's more permanent than words. I said I was sorry and that Tamsyn would negotiate a severance package. I assumed, wrongly as it turns out, that Amanda would want out.

AMANDA: The package was pitiful. If I was only going to live six months it would have been fine, but I intend to live longer than that.

BRYONY: Tamsyn researched it thoroughly and assured me it was fair.

BRIAN: This hasn't come to the Board either.

BRYONY: It's very recent, Brian.

BRIAN: What's the package being proposed?
TAMSYN: [*looking embarrassed*] Twenty weeks pay.
BRIAN: After how many years service?
AMANDA: Twenty-seven.
BRIAN: That's not exactly what I'd call generous.
TAMSYN: [*looking at* BRYONY] I'm only too happy to go back and look at it again.
BRIAN: Bryony, I'm starting to feel we have a real problem here with your executive team. Cassie is months late giving us a much-needed financial snapshot of how we're travelling because she can't master a piece of software, Giulia failed to head off a public relations disaster over little Katrina, and along with Cassie came up with a plan that might have led to an even greater disaster, and Tamsyn here recommends a severance package that would make Ebenezer Scrooge look like a spendthrift.
BRYONY: I have to say, Brian, that for the last couple of months I've started to share your doubts, but I appointed them all and the buck stops with me.
BRIAN: I'm sorry to have to say it, Bryony, but yes it does.
BRYONY: Tamsyn, I don't know where you came up with that figure, but it *is* far too low.
TAMSYN: I'm sorry.
BRIAN: You're all very quick to say 'sorry', but these are all very serious and substantial mistakes.
BRYONY: [*to* TAMSYN] Could you research this again much more thoroughly and come back to me as soon as possible with another figure?

    TAMSYN *nods, with a set angry face.*

BRIAN: [*to* TAMSYN] Where did you find that figure? I simply can't believe an experienced Human Resources Director could be that uniformed or callous.
TAMSYN: [*suddenly angry*] Bryony. Can't you be honest just for once?! [*To* BRIAN] The truth is I recommended a much higher figure. I *am* a professional. I know what the rates should be. Bryony just said no. Twenty weeks was it?!
BRYONY: Tamsyn, that's a lie.
TAMSYN: You know damn well it's not a lie. Fire me if you want. I just can't sit here and be blamed for things I didn't do.

GIULIA: Me either! I did go to Bryony with the plan to send Katrina's family on a holiday. I even had them booked into Hayman Island. And Bryony said no. 'Katrina's family were the type that made loud threats and did nothing', she said.

BRYONY: I can't believe you're saying this, Giulia.

CASSIE: And it wasn't Giulia and my idea to change our whole orientation to this new talent spotting scheme.

GIULIA: [*to* BRYONY] It was yours.

CASSIE: You called us into your office and told us.

BRYONY: We developed it together and you were both very, very enthusiastic.

GIULIA: At the start.

CASSIE: But then we started having second thoughts and you wouldn't listen.

BRYONY: Well, your doubts must have been spoken very softly because I didn't hear them.

GIULIA: They weren't voiced as strongly as we should've because, let's face it, who would dare?

CASSIE: Look what happened to Amanda.

TAMSYN: And just for the record, Amanda's no more paranoid than I am. Bryony came to see me and asked my advice on how to make her life as uncomfortable as possible.

BRYONY: That is a straight-out lie.

TAMSYN: Fire me, Bryony. I'm sick of it. Look, I thought Amanda was a problem, but I shouldn't have let myself become party to a systematically plotted torture process.

AMANDA: Thank God someone's finally admitted it.

BRIAN: You were a willing party to this process, Tamsyn?

TAMSYN: Like Cassie said. You don't voice objections to Bryony.

BRYONY: Don't try and act the innocent, Tamsyn. You wanted her out of there as much as I did. After the cat incident you came bounding into my office with a huge grin on your face and said, 'We've got her'.

TAMSYN: Okay. I became part of the game. It was like school again. All the 'in' group victimising the outcast. It's insidious with someone like Bryony around. Even Stella joined in eventually.

AMANDA: In the back of my mind I always knew it was true, but after so *many* denials, you start to think you're mad.

BRYONY: Brian, this is total hysteria. Amanda was under-performing. The Board wouldn't let me fire her. What alternative did I have but to nudge her in that direction?

TAMSYN: It was a witch hunt and you know it. And I'm ashamed I was part of it.

AMANDA: Somebody finally admits it.

TAMSYN: [*to* AMANDA] The plan was to get rid of you, then turn the heat up on Stella.

STELLA: I should've known.

TAMSYN: I really knew I'd backed the wrong horse when I told Bryony that Amanda had breast cancer, and she said—

BRYONY: Tamsyn, you've really said enough.

TAMSYN: She said, 'Everyone has to die sometime'.

CASSIE: And just so you know, Brian, there's no problem with the software. The problem is with what the software shows.

BRIAN: Which is what?

CASSIE: The impact of the Katrina fiasco has been huge. People don't like us, don't trust us, and our net income has fallen by something like nineteen percent.

    BRIAN *stares at* BRYONY.

BRIAN: We'll either have to cancel some of our programs or go into massive debt.

CASSIE: Precisely.

BRYONY: We've had a setback, Brian, which I didn't want to bring to the Board until I had a contingency plan in place to cope. The scholarship scheme, being a lower cost option, was one of those plans. I've got others and please remember we should be thinking long term. The new television appeal featuring little Jill and I has already tested very strongly in our market research. Brian, five or ten years down the track the policies I've put in place will deliver. I can assure you of that. And today has been very valuable to me. The real enemy to E and C achieving its goals is not Amanda. Not even Stella. It's these three here.

    She points to GIULIA, TAMSYN *and* CASSIE.

And I'm not just talking about their refusal to accept responsibility for their part in the recent errors in judgement, I'm talking about their basic skills. All three have to go. And, Brian, I'm not tolerating any more obstructionism at Board level. They go or I go.

GIULIA: Bryony. We're not the problem, you are.

BRYONY: [*suddenly snapping and attacking them viciously*] It's about time someone told you three the truth. I've been covering for your deficiencies for far too long. Giulia, you are a *total* disappointment. Your media contacts and clout are pathetic, and you haven't put in a fraction of the effort needed to improve them. Cassie, your financial skills are appalling for someone supposedly qualified to your level, and your personal and social skills are even more appalling. Tamsyn, you've been promoted way above your level of competence already and you're a total embarrassment. If I had one word of advice for all three of you it would be to find someone rich and get married, because you're all headed nowhere professionally.

BRYONY *looks back at* BRIAN, *then is suddenly calm again.*

Brian, I can deliver, believe me. I can and will deliver, but I'll have no more obstruction at Board level. These five go or I go. There's got to be a wholesale rebuilding from the ground up. Give me your backing and give me the resources and E and C will be the pacesetter for the next fifty years. Now if you don't mind this has taken up enough time, so I'm heading back to the office to do what I've been paid to do, and when you get in touch with the Board and confirm that I've got their full backing then call me.

She gets up to go and turns back to JACK.

Thank you, Jack. This has proved most helpful.

She leaves. They stare after her in silence.

JACK: Brian, I've got the feeling you've got a bit of a problem here.

BRIAN: Yes. Amanda, on behalf of the Board I apologise. Sincerely.

AMANDA: Thank you.

BRIAN: If you want to retire, a fair package will be arranged.

AMANDA: I might be a bit wonky during the chemo, but I want to keep working.

BRIAN *nods, then looks at* TAMSYN, CASSIE *and* GIULIA.

BRIAN: I'm not sure the Board's going to be all that much more impressed with you three than with Bryony.

CASSIE: We couldn't stand up to her. No one could. She'd go ballistic. You just saw it.
JACK: If it's of any interest, I chased up some people who worked under Bryony in her previous jobs.
STELLA: And?
JACK: She's a dead-set bully. Rules by terror everywhere she's been. She reduced her last two organisations to a shambles too.
STELLA: Why didn't the Board know that, Brian?
JACK: They wrote her marvellous references to get rid of her.
BRIAN: We made enquiries. I never trust written references.
STELLA: You couldn't have enquired too deeply.
BRIAN: We knew she was controversial and abrasive, but we felt we needed someone tough in there after Alan.
STELLA: Brian, whatever you decide, I won't be staying around if Bryony is.
BRIAN: She won't be.
STELLA: And I won't be around if these three are, either.
AMANDA: Neither will I.
GIULIA: Amanda, we wouldn't be the same if Bryony was gone.
AMANDA: Giulia, there's been too much pain.
BRIAN: Frankly the chances of you three staying on here range from zilch to very small.
CASSIE: That's not fair.
BRIAN: Look, you're all bright, you're all young, and if you've learned something from this you could all be headed for brilliant careers. But not here.
STELLA: What *is* going to happen, Brian?
BRIAN: I'll have to talk it over with the Board. At length. And try and see if we can salvage something from this disaster. [*He gets up and moves towards the door.*] Thanks Jack. I'm not sure what for.
JACK: Clarification?

> BRIAN *sighs and leaves.* TAMSYN *tries to say something to* AMANDA, *but can't and leaves with her head down.* GIULIA *comes across and faces* AMANDA *and finally is able to drag out what she wants to say.*

GIULIA: [*to* AMANDA] It was like she was a witch and had us in her spell. I hope the chemo's successful.

CASSIE: Me too.

AMANDA *nods.* GIULIA *and* CASSIE *hurry away.*

STELLA: I'm sorry too, Mandy. I really am.

AMANDA *nods. They hug.*

So what's going to happen, Jack?

JACK: You want my guess? The Board won't go back to the modest and simple direct mail appeal days. Not with Brian as Chair of the Board. The big sell and high pressure are still going to feel like the future to him. He'll just decide he chose the wrong CEO and bring in the headhunters to find the next one, who sure as eggs'll be another bully and your lives probably won't be all that much better.

STELLA: Thanks a lot.

JACK: And he'll give Bryony a glowing reference so she'll agree to let him break her contract, and she'll be very quickly snapped up by some other outfit for her 'tough', 'hard-hitting', 'no prisoners' approach, and in two or three years will have 'delivered similar results' to yet another organisation.

STELLA: You're really fun to have around, Jack.

JACK: You asked.

AMANDA: I'm amazed that boards don't work out that these bullies are counterproductive?

JACK: A lot of them do. But not when they're headed up by someone like Brian who still thinks that kicking heads is the way the world works. Of course there's a slight chance that the rest of the Board might rebel and appoint someone who knows the difference between firmness and bluster. And who listens and values the contributions of others. And is fair, just and inspiring.

STELLA: But probably not.

JACK: Have a few lunches with your contact and the chances might improve. [*To* AMANDA] When's your next bout of chemo?

AMANDA: Two weeks.

JACK: They say it's not nice.

AMANDA: It's terrible.

JACK: All the best. You should both apply for the top job yourselves.

STELLA: I'm going to.

AMANDA *looks at her in surprise.*

They won't give it to me, but at least it'll embarrass them into thinking about why not. Coming, Amanda?

AMANDA: If you're going to apply, I am too.

STELLA: Good. Thanks Jack.

JACK: I didn't do much. Like most narcissists, Bryony finally dug her own grave.

> STELLA *nods and goes.*

AMANDA: I feel as if I've just come out of a long, dark tunnel.

JACK: I'm very glad.

> AMANDA *nods, smiles and goes.* JACK *watches her go out the door and packs his papers into his briefcase. He sees something on the table. It's the photo of little Jill that Bryony has left there. He picks it up, looks at it, shrugs, then puts it back. He leaves.*

THE END

ALSO BY DAVID WILLIAMSON FROM CURRENCY

After the Ball
Brilliant Lies
The Club
Collected Plays: Volume I
Collected Plays: Volume II
Dead White Males
The Department
Don's Party
Emerald City
The Great Man / Sanctuary
Money and Friends
The Perfectionist
The Removalists
Siren
Son's of Cain
Third World Blues
Top Silk
Travelling North
Up For Grabs/Corporate Vibes

ABOUT DAVID WILLIAMSON

Brian Kiernan, *David Williamson: A Writer's Career*
This authoritative account of Williamson's phenomenal career draws on his early writings, unpublished drafts, letters and journal entries; as well as the recollections of his friends and colleagues.

COMING SOON

David B. Moore, *The Jack Manning Trilogy, A Study Guide*
The guide is designed to help teachers use the plays more effectively in the classroom whether it be from a literary, theatrical or counselling perspective. The guide is written by David Moore, a founding director of TJA (Transformative Justice Australia), the Sydney-based company that inspired Williamson's trilogy. David taught at the University of Melbourne and Charles Sturt University, then worked as a government adviser. Since 1995, he has worked internationally, bringing TJA conferencing to workplaces, the justice system, and schools. David has worked extensively with schools in Australia and North America to design conflict management programs. He also works frequently with professional actors to dramatise aspects of TJA's work. Available in May.

For a full list of our titles, visit our website:
www.currency.com.au

Currency Press
The performing arts publisher
Gadigal Land, Suite 310
46–56 Kippax Street,
Surry Hills NSW 2010
Australia
enquiries@currency.com.au
Tel: (02) 9319 5877

www.ingramcontent.com/pod-product-compliance
Lightning Source LLC
Chambersburg PA
CBHW040306170426
43194CB00022B/2919